Harboring Happiness
101 Ways To Be Happy

Dan Brook, PhD

For information, or to order additional copies, please
contact:

Beacon Publishing Group
P.O. Box 41573 Charleston, S.C. 29423
800.817.8480| beaconpublishinggroup.com

Publisher's catalog available by request.

ISBN-13: 978-1-949472-32-5

ISBN-10: 1-949472-32-5

Published in 2021. New York, NY 10001.

First Edition. Printed in the USA.

Dedicated to all those already happy
to all those who want to be,
and to all those on the way.

Praise for *Harboring Happiness*

"A delightful collection of essential practices to help us nourish our natural capacity for happiness. A gem of a book!"

> — Tara Brach, PhD, author of *Radical Acceptance* and *Radical Compassion*

"This is a fantastic, practical, and succinct summary of evidence-based — and heartfelt, inspired — ways to cultivate resilient well-being in stressful times. What a beautiful book!"

> — Rick Hanson, PhD, author of *Neurodharma: New Science, Ancient Wisdom* and *Seven Practices of the Highest Happiness*

"This is a wonderful, useful, and inspiring book. What Dr. Dan Brook reveals will change your individual mind and relationships. A delight for us all."

> — Dacher Keltner, PhD, Co-Director of the Greater Good Science Center at the University of California, Berkeley and author of *Born to Be Good* and co-author of *Understanding Emotions*

"To be frank, I was a bit discomfited to see another book on happiness; particularly in this time of COVID. But this book is different. Dr. Brook's *Harboring Happiness* provides a kaleidoscopic tour that is as informative as it is a delight to read. Combining substantive evidence-backed commentary with witty and lucid prose, this book made me smile. I took solace not only in Dr. Brook's sound advice about happiness, but for its implications for a more meaningful life. So if you're searching for a richer, livelier, and more sustainable existence, this book is for you!"

— Kirk Schneider, PhD, President of the Existential-Humanistic Institute and author of *The Spirituality of Awe* and *The Depolarizing of America: A Guidebook for Social Healing*

Introduction

You *can* be happy. You can also skip this introduction and go straight to the happiness techniques. It's your book, your life, and your rules. The choices are yours, too.

Mark Victor Hansen, co-author of the *Chicken Soup for the Soul* books, advises you to "Dedicate yourself to the good you deserve and desire for yourself. Give yourself peace of mind. You deserve to be happy. You deserve delight." This is true no matter who or what or where you are!

Photo by Daniel Xavier

Happiness is a psychological and sociological skill — even if there might also be biological, genetic, and neurological components. The interdisciplinary science of happiness teaches us that it is a set of skills you can learn, practice, increase, share, and enjoy.

Indeed, Sonja Lyubomirsky's research in her *The How of Happiness* indicates that half our happiness may be due to genetics, only 10% to life circumstances, and 40%, the part we can control, to our thoughts and actions. Lyubomirsky writes that "Our intentional, effortful activities have a powerful effect on how happy we are, over and above the effects of our [genetic] set points and the circumstances in which we find ourselves."

William Arthur Ward realized: "Happiness is an inside job." Although there might not be a *specific* recipe for your happiness, there are a variety of ingredients for you to choose from and combine in this little book.

Stanford University researcher Emma Seppälä discovered that we do not become happy because we are successful; we are more likely to be successful in *anything* because we are happy. "When we value our happiness — and also the happiness of those around us — we become more productive, more focused, more resilient, more charismatic, and more influential — not to mention more innovative, too.," she explains. "The ability to have fun improves our relationships, helping us connect with our colleagues, family, and friends more easily, and even makes us more attractive to others."

Writing about awe, which can increase our happiness, humanistic psychologist Kirk Schneider distinguishes between a "quick boil" of happiness and a "slow simmer" of joy. This dichotomy also arises in my "A Sociology of Joy."

One does not need to be *constantly* happy — an impossibility — to have a joyful life. Whether we think of it as happiness, joy, bliss, excitement, contentment, wellbeing, or satisfaction, it has to be much more than a flash in the pan that quickly comes and goes. We should strive to make happiness a process and a lifestyle.

Albert Einstein preferred the joyous slow simmer: "A calm and modest life bring much more happiness than constantly chasing success, which always involves constant restlessness." Likewise, French Tibetan Buddhist monk Matthieu Ricard, a former biochemist who has been described as the "world's happiest man," remarks that "Happiness is not an endless succession of pleasurable feelings; it's an exceptionally healthy way of living."

Also for Aristotle, happiness, just like excellence in *anything*, is not about a moment, thing, position, possession, event, feeling, hope, person, job, or distant promise. Based on Aristotle's eudemonia, happiness is a process, a practice, a habit. To put it in the words of my LinkedIn acquaintance Felix Aiwekhoe: "If you sow bitterness, you will harvest bitterness...and if you sow happiness, you will harvest happiness."

Writing from prison during World War I, revolutionary Rosa Luxemburg recognized that "When one has the bad habit of looking for a drop of poison in any blossom, one finds good reason, as long as one lives, to be moaning and groaning ... If you take the opposite approach, and look for the honey in every blossom, then you'll always find reasons to be cheerful." Being miserable, sad, angry, resentful, etc. is as much a habit as being happy, cheerful, and content. In that vein, Google's Mo Gawdat, who wrote *Solve for Happy*, advises us to "make happiness a priority" and to "develop happiness skills." I hope you find some here and put them to use.

Whatever your thoughts and feelings about happiness, here are 101 possible paths backed by science to help get you there.

1.
Earn enough to cover all your needs and some wants

People are much more likely to be happy after they have their basic needs met, at least some of their wants, and a savings cushion for just-in-case scenarios. Decreased financial anxiety is likely to lead to increased happiness. However, happiness no longer increases with additional income or stuff (even "awesome stuff") for people who live in wealthier countries. The opposite can be said for those in poorer countries.

Reggae singer Bob Marley offered invaluable insight: "money is numbers and numbers never end. If it takes money to be happy, your search for happiness will never end." That said, people are happy *and* unhappy at all income levels in all countries, though people tend to be happier in more egalitarian countries with higher average incomes.

Dan Brook, PhD

2.
Get more experiences

People who get more experiences—travel, road trips, concerts, theatre, restaurants, hiking, camping, picnics, movies, museums, classes, games, events, outings, conversations, dancing, hobbies, learning new skills, exploring neighborhoods—tend to enjoy those activities and then continue to enjoy them as they reminisce about them.

It is "better to do than to have" because "experiences have a longer-lasting effect on happiness." This is especially true of new, exciting, or unique experiences, including peak experiences. According to psychologist Abraham Maslow, these are ones that are "rare, exciting, oceanic, deeply moving, exhilarating, elevating experiences that generate an advanced form of perceiving reality."

Variety plays a role. "Spending my money on experiences brings me so much more joy than spending it on material possessions," Charissa Enget shared through Quora. "I'm a lot happier and stress free without them." Charissa decided to get her master's degree in engineering in Thailand after growing up in America.

Some physical things, though, can also act like experiences—especially certain photos, art, colorfully-painted walls, electronics, souvenirs, toys, heirlooms, etc.

3.
Collect fewer things

We all need things, as we are physical beings living in a physical world. But, material things tend to weigh us down. The more things we have, the more things we have to organize, guard, and defend. Physically. Cognitively. Emotionally. In this sense, property becomes a sort of prison, as what we own also owns us.

Roman emperor and Stoic philosopher Marcus Aurelius had careful words around possessions: "remember this: that very little is needed to make a happy life." Prior to him, Socrates opined that "the secret of happiness, you see, is not found in seeking more, but in developing the capacity to enjoy less." In modern times, Rabbi Hyman Schachtel reveals that the secret to happiness is not necessarily having what you want but wanting what you have.

4.

Maintain and increase your health

Don't simply survive: thrive! Health is wealth, and one's health is essential to one's happiness. Ancient Roman poet Juvenal recommended *"mens sana in corpore sano"*: having a healthy mind in a healthy body. Therefore, we should emphasize plant-based diets without too much processed food-like products (good food leads to a good mood!), hydration (we are mostly water, after all), exercise (use it or lose it), social relationships (family and friends), and staying away from smoke and other toxic pollutants. All are all good for health and happiness.

These practices are some of the commonalities of Blue Zones, the several places in the world where communities of people live the longest and are disproportionately centenarians. Meditation (returning to yourself and relaxing, whether secular or religious) and sleep (rejuvenation) are also beneficial for health and happiness.

Because there is such a close connection between health and happiness, making sure you have health coverage and access to healthcare is vitally important. Further, it is best when a society has a universal system so that everyone is guaranteed healthcare. The societies that have universal healthcare tend to be the healthiest and happiest countries.

5.

Be around friends and others who make you happy

"Friends make our lives happier," writes Sandip Roy. A 75-year study at Harvard University had one clear message: " Good relationships keep us happier and healthier." There are different types of friends and levels of friendship for different times, places, and purposes, but they are important for our happiness. "People's happiness depends on the happiness of others with whom they are connected." In contrast, we have discovered that "loneliness is bad for your health."

Other studies find that happiness is contagious, just as many other emotions and behaviors are, making them at least as sociological as they are psychological. Jon Krakauer has said that "happiness [is] only real when shared" and sharing with friends makes us healthier and happier. Further, social isolation for members of a social species like ours can be as deadly as obesity or being sedentary. Social connections are a key to a happy life.

6.
Love

Feeling love for another, receiving love, and expressing love are all happiness drugs. The mystic Rumi recommended to "close your eyes, fall in love, and stay there." A good marriage or other romantic relationship is a big boost to happiness. "There is only one happiness in life," George Sand declared, "to love and be loved." Santa Barbara City Councilor Babatunde Folayemi wisely realized that it is not enough to love others, but also to safely allow others to love you.

Even lovingkindness exercises—for example, wishing good things, peace, health, happiness, etc. for others—boosts one's happiness.

7.
Minimize social media and TV

Social media can lead to internet addiction and depression. "When researchers measured the welfare of hundreds of people who left Facebook for a month, they found the people were happier...[and] more active in real-life activities." Digital distancing is good for happiness. Although too much screen time is not good, none might not be good either for many people. Experts now believe, based on a study of one million teenagers, that about one hour of screen time per day is most likely to lead to happiness (with exceptions for activities like school, work, writing, coding, creating art, donating, connecting with loved ones, etc.).

Each time you focus on a screen—for a text, ping, message, email, call, TV show, video game, whatever—you are declaring that to be the *most* important thing in the world to you. The prioritization of your screen becomes more important than whoever you are with, anything anybody is saying, whatever you are doing, and anything you might have been thinking about. Addictions are not healthy and decrease happiness, so it is best to find ways to limit your screen time and do something else you enjoy instead. "Seriously," Eric Barker asks us, "how many of the best moments of your life happened in front of a screen?"

"Research at the University of Pittsburgh School of Medicine concluded that social media usage and depression have a symbiotic relationship. Turn off your screen and start living your own life, not vicariously through others." And as Stephen Covey reminds us, "the main thing is to keep the main thing the main thing" and the main thing is very rarely on the screen.

8.
Avoid advertisements

Advertisements are an especially dangerous form of media. Some have called them anti-therapy, as they are designed to trick and manipulate us while getting us to feel bad about ourselves and our lives.

Advertisements have been said to be "killing us softly," while encouraging us to consume things we don't necessarily need nor want, can't necessarily afford, aren't necessarily healthy, and probably are not sustainable. Advertising is simply a form of brainwashing to achieve and maximize corporate profit, regardless of personal, social, and environmental consequences—including our happiness.

Choose your brainwashing consciously and carefully!

9.

Get more good news!

There is plenty of bad news in the world, and we sometimes might need to know about it. There is also a *lot* of good news out there, though we are less likely to hear about it for a variety of reasons. Decrease some of the bad news in your life while also increasing more of the good news!

Seek out the good on InspireMore, Happify Daily, Daily Good, Good News Network, The Optimist Daily, karunavirus, Good, Positive News, and other sources. Corinne Sanders states that good news has research-backed benefits: "it boosts your mood and outlook."

10.
Don't compare yourself to others

It depends on who or what your reference group is, but we socially compare ourselves upward to an idealized individual or group that we superficially *think* is in one or more ways better than us *way* too often. This practice typically leads to feelings of relative deprivation, inferiority, disappointment, and unhappiness.

Fascinating studies of Olympic champions show that bronze medal winners are typically happier than silver medal winners because silver medalists compare up to gold medal winners and feel the loss. Bronze medal winners compare down to non-winners and feel the win. "Comparison is the killer of happiness," according to Mathieu Ricard. Others have said that "comparison is the thief of joy."

Get perspective and be comfortable with yourself. We are not in competition with others, not even with ourselves. We should be happy for other people's circumstances, happiness, and success, as well as our own, whether real or perceived. When we do, we will be happier.

11.
Emphasize your positives, de-emphasize your negatives

As important as it is to reduce negativities in one's life—and it really is—it is *even more* crucial to increase the positives in our lives. "My life has been full of terrible misfortunes," Michel de Montaigne recalled in the sixteenth century," most of which never happened."

Do more of what you love, emphasizing the good while de-emphasizing the bad! This is as true of your personal qualities as it is about the things you do.

12.

Watch videos that make you smile and laugh

Whether it's comedies or cats—or *whatever* works for you—adding more funny things into your life will allow you to smile and laugh more. Therefore, you'll enjoy your life more.

You shouldn't be embarrassed about your smiling and laughing; you should be proud of them and show them off!

13.

Smile and laugh, whether you have a reason or not

Smiling can be powerful medicine. Happy thoughts not only are more likely to lead to smiling, but smiling is more likely to lead to happy thoughts. "Sometimes your joy is the source of your smile," Buddhist monk Thich Nhat Hanh relates. "But sometimes your smile can be the source of your joy," as well as other people's joy.

Laura Ingalls Wilder reminds us about the power of laughter, a trait that likely precedes language: "a good laugh overcomes more difficulties and dissipates more dark clouds than any other one thing." Some people practice smile meditation and laughter yoga with happy results, which is actually pretty funny.

14.
Listen to your music

Music activates special parts of our brains. Up-tempo music in a major key makes us especially feel good. So, turn up the tunes.

Try the Partridge Family's "Come On Get Happy," Bobby McFerrin's "Don't Worry Be Happy," Pharrell Williams' "Happy," and Michael Franti's "Enjoy Every Second," to name a few!

There are *lots* of other happy songs, whether explicitly or not. If it makes *you* happy, it's the right music! And you can make your own music. For example, singing can also be a happiness boost, regardless of your level of talent.

15.
Express gratitude

Gratitude is the gift we give when we receive gifts. Whether we realize it or not, we have always received and are *always* receiving material and non-material gifts!

Brené Brown told Oprah that "in 12 years of research, I have never interviewed a single person with the capacity to really experience joy who does not also actively practice gratitude." Yale University professor Laurie Santos teaches the school's most popular course: the Science of Well-Being, She reports that "gratitude is a killer of envy."

Being grateful does not mean we are not aware of whatever might be bad; it simply means we appreciate the good and do not simply take it for granted. "Being happy doesn't mean the day is perfect," according to my LinkedIn friend Felix Aiwekhoe, "it only means you have decided to overlook the imperfection of the day."

Having an attitude of gratitude, especially after we savor whatever it is we are grateful for, is associated with having a joyful life. Keeping a gratitude journal or maintaining a gratitude list can be helpful and fun.

16.
Practice random acts of kindness

Doing a kind thing for someone else is also one of the kindest things you can do for yourself. "The best way to cheer yourself up," Mark Twain once quipped, "is to try to cheer someone else up." Martin Luther King, Jr. similarly said "the surest way to be happy is to seek happiness for others." Being kind boosts your health and happiness.

Experiment with acts of kindness that are small and large, social and financial, symbolic and actual, verbal and physical. Do *at least* one of these every day. As has been said, "giving is a form of receiving." Even better than random acts of kindness are organized, purposeful, intentional, and systematic acts of kindness! "Happiness held is the seed," according to John Harrigan, while "happiness shared is the flower."

17.
Manage stress

Stress is a normal and necessary part of life, allowing us to react and survive as individuals and as a species. Getting *stressed out*, however, is unfortunate and unnecessary. When we experience stress, our bodies release adrenalin and cortisol, which are useful in the short-term for fight or fright.

We begin swimming in these stress hormones and remain in constant crisis mode. It's a toxic state for our minds and bodies. So, don't get stuck in the needless anxiety of what Dr. Rick Hanson calls "paper tiger paranoia": those daily things which can seem scary, but really aren't.

We cannot control the external, but we *can* control the internal. It is not possible to eliminate stress, so we need to develop a better relationship with it that allows us to more effectively manage our it—instead of allowing it to manage us. This is true not just of major stressors, but also of the many instances of inconvenience, annoyance, and micro-stress throughout our days.

There are many ways to effectively manage stress. Resilience, sometimes referred to as grit, is an important antidote to stress and a critical path to happiness. So is perspective. And, of course, various other pathways in this book.

18.
Meditate

I first met a friend of mine in Thailand after he had been a monk for 17 years. He says he meditates to have a peaceful mind, and having a peaceful mind makes him happy. There are *many* kinds of meditation and many ways to meditate: one could focus on the breath, on a mantra, on compassion for others, on smiling or laughing, even on kittens, and you can do it anywhere and in any position. I also engage in micro-meditation. Simply being in silence for a couple of minutes can be beneficial.

Distinguished psychologist Daniel Goleman says that metta (lovingkindness) meditation also has positive effects. This is where one thinks positive thoughts for oneself and/or others, which can include repeating a positive mantra. "It turns out that the repetition of those phrases is psychoactive; it actually changes the brain and how you feel right from the get-go. We find, for example, that people who do this meditation... are kinder, they are more likely to help someone in need, they're more generous, and they're happier. It turns out that the brain areas that help us or that make us want to help someone that we care about also connect with the circuitry for feeling good."

Experiment with different forms of meditation to find the ones that work best for you in different times and circumstances. The best meditative practice, as is often advised, is the one you will actually do.

Dan Brook, PhD

19.
Practice compassion

Practice compassion for others.

Be sympathetic, wish them well, assume they have struggles. We all do as we move along our life paths. Practicing compassion for others can reduce anger, resentment, and other negative thoughts and emotions, giving us more space and capacity to be happy, which makes it a great gift.

Indeed, the Dalai Lama says with his signature laugh, "if you want *others* to be happy, practice compassion. If *you* want to be happy, practice compassion."

20.
Practice self-compassion

Because you are a person in this world, you also need to practice compassion for yourself. Too many of us are extremely and unnecessarily harsh on ourselves, yet part of having compassion is having self-compassion.

We frequently pick on ourselves, physically and emotionally. If we spoke to our friends the way we sometimes speak to ourselves, they would not remain our friends. If our friends regularly spoke to us the way we speak to ourselves, we would not be friends with them anymore, thinking that they are sadistic sociopaths. We would be right.

Be kind to yourself, the way you probably are to your friends and the way you would want other people to treat you. Self-compassion and self-love are about the Bronze Rule: do unto yourself as you would do unto those you love the most and do not do unto yourself as you would not want others to do unto you.

How you engage in the world starts with you, so be kind, compassionate, and loving to yourself. That way, we can make the world happier for both ourselves and others.

Dan Brook, PhD

21.
Engage in service

"Happiness cannot be pursued," Holocaust survivor Dr. Viktor Frankl asserts, "it must ensue, and it only does so as the unintended side effect of one's personal dedication to a cause greater than oneself or as the by-product of one's surrender to a person other than oneself." Ndukwe Kalu puts it another way: "the things you do for yourself are gone when you are gone, but the things you do for others remain as your legacy."

Serving others through volunteering is an excellent way to create meaning and social change—and possibly feel the "helper's high" or "warm glow" that creates a more joyful life. A Harvard Health study concluded that "weekly volunteering leads to happiness levels comparable to a life-changing salary boost." For many people, serving other people is one of the best ways to serve themselves.

You can also donate some of your time, money, things, labor, skills, attention, or space to help others, which will improve your community *and* your level of happiness. "If you light a lamp for someone else," the Buddha taught, "it will also brighten your path." And as Zen master Thich Nhat

Hanh says: "if you give and continue to give, you become richer and richer all the time, richer in terms of happiness and well-being." Mahatma Gandhi went so far as to say that "the best way to find yourself is to lose yourself in the service of others."

22.
Think of others

Thinking of others is a great way to think and feel better about yourself. "Rather than dismissing or criticizing when you see a stranger," advises Geoffrey James, "bring a kind thought or a positive idea into your mind."

Even if it remains in the realm of thought, simply thinking well of others will lead to happier thoughts in yourself. Some people do this when they hear sirens—ambulances, fire trucks, police cars, alarms, bells—thinking of and wishing the best for whoever might need it at that moment.

23.
Banish envy, jealousy, and ...

Envy and jealousy, like regret and worry, are *worse* than useless.

Not only do they not ever accomplish anything positive or constructive—but, rather, they are toxic feelings that sap our energy, increase our stress, and lead to unhappiness. "Positive thinking," Zig Ziglar noticed, "will let you do everything better than negative thinking."

Free yourselves from these wasteful negativities and embrace your happier self.

24.
Forgive

Forgiveness is important because it frees us from a huge burden and breeds happiness, regardless of what's happened in the past. Forgiveness allows us to let go of the anger, resentment, grudge, disappointment, and injury without condoning the past behavior or allowing it to continue with us.

Offering forgiveness demonstrates compassion and can be therapeutic; to request forgiveness can sometimes be selfish and cruel. Forgiving is more foe-giving than forgetting, giving away the past foes to one's happiness, even if we continue to remember them. Forgiveness is a path to peace.

"Forgiveness does not change the past," Paul Boese counsels, "but it does enlarge the future" by not letting past trauma steal our present and future happiness. Forgiving others is not necessarily for *their* benefit, but for ours—and we deserve it. "Forgiveness," Byron Katie declares, "is just another name for freedom." Forgiving ourselves for whatever wrongs we committed in the past, whether to ourselves or others, is just as powerful and necessary.

25.

Mindfulness

Mindfulness is heightened mental alertness, awareness of present experience with acceptance and a focus on the here and now—wherever and whatever it is. When we successfully do so, we are not wallowing in the past nor worrying about the future. With mindfulness, we are simply enjoying the gift of the present.

During one of my hikes in Colorado, I noticed that Grizzly Creek was flowing along its course over rocks, boulders, trees, branches, and whatever else was in its path, yet the creek flowed regardless. It didn't complain, it didn't blame, it didn't begrudge, it didn't make excuses. It simply flowed. And when it was blocked one way, it went another. The creek quite often went *around*, but also beautifully *over*, creating little waterfalls whenever necessary. Obstacles, temperature, weather, scenery, wildlife, people—all did not matter. The water not only did what it needed to do, it did what was *easiest* to do. Water never goes where it cannot, yet it always effortlessly goes where it can. We can too.

26.
Reach out, touch some-one...and be touched

Humans are a social species. Skin-to-skin contact—touching and being touched—can make people happier when done under the right circumstances. Consensual hugging, touching, holding hands, giving and getting massages, high fives, kissing, cuddling, snuggling, and other forms of touching are all great ways for a social species like humans to feel happier—though certainly not for everyone.

Paul Zak, PhD, Director of the Center for Neuroeconomics Studies at Claremont Graduate University, reveals "a number of studies show that when people touch you, your brain produces oxytocin." This powerful brain hormone relates to social bonding, relationships, and love. Tiffany Field, PhD, founder of the Touch Research Institute at the University of Miami School of Medicine, also says that "touch lowers the production of the stress hormone cortisol."

These types of warm fuzzies can—and should—be received from humans *and* non-humans. Use the power of touch to boost your mood.

27.

Capture "thin slices of joy"

Google's former Happiness Guru Chade-Meng Tan recommends noticing small and mundane things that are nice or pleasant. According to Tan, there is a 3-step process to build a habit: "a trigger, a routine, and a reward." "The trigger… is the pleasant moment, the routine is the noticing of it, and the reward is the feeling of joy itself." We can capture a few seconds of happiness with these steps and doing them often adds up to a happier life. Achieving and celebrating small accomplishments adds more happiness to our lives.

Samuel Taylor Coleridge realized that "the happiness of life is made up of minute fractions, the soon forgotten charities of a kiss, a smile, a kind look, a gentle word, a heartfelt compliment." Maria Shriver refers to these phenomena as "yippee moments." In a way, this is an old idea.

Zeno, the founder of the ancient Greek philosophy of Stoicism, commented that "well-being is realized by small steps, but is truly no small thing." Some people call it baby steps, mini-habits, or micro-changes; the Japanese call it *kaizen*, a growth mindset of small, continuous, positive changes in one's life.

If you make it a habit to appreciate the little things, and especially if you savor them at the time, you will find that the little things in life become the big things in life.

28.
Get exercise

Exercise gets blood pumping to your heart and brain, releasing endorphins that can boost your mood and strengthen your body. Any way you move your body is a good way: aerobics, dancing, sports, walking, running, hiking, biking, swimming, yoga, tai chi, qi gong, martial arts, CrossFit, HIIT, treadmill, elliptical, weight training, jumping, skipping, whatever.

In addition to being good for your physical health and longevity, exercise is associated with better looks, better cognition, and better mood. So, get moving and get happier as you get more fit.

29.

Have sex at least once per week

Whether you need another excuse to have more sex or another reason to be happy, people who have sex at least once a week tend to be happier. So, have at it. Two or three times a week is even better, and everyday might be best!

Sex is good for physical health, mental health, spiritual health, and your relationships. If you don't have a partner, you always have yourself.

Feminist Gloria Steinem recommended to graduating students in her 2017 Commencement Address to "have sex, fun, and laughter." Hugs, kisses, and holding hands are also very beneficial and fun!

30.
Enjoy your hobbies, do what you enjoy, pursue meaningful activities

Make time for the activities you enjoy, even if you are busy. Perhaps *especially* if you are busy. If necessary, build them into your schedule to make sure to get to do the things you enjoy. This relates to the Japanese concept of *ikigai*, a purpose in life, and the Costa Rican *plan de vida*, reason for living, sometimes described as a motivation to get up in the morning.

Having a sense of purpose, a goal, or something you derive meaning from is associated with happiness. Pursue a purpose bigger than yourself. As Joan Baez once said, "action is the antidote to despair."

There is always room for more positive activities, even more so after decreasing negative activities. The best hobbies for happiness are projects and passions that are meaningful to you, those that you can make progress on, and those that can make a difference in some way.

Author and activist Rebecca Solnit recognizes that "disconnection from a larger sense of purpose and agency, from community and civil society, and from hope are huge factors in unhappiness." Albert Einstein's advice was this: "if you want to live a happy life, tie it to a goal, not to people or things."

31.
Excite yourself!

Doing new and exciting activities is good for your happiness. Chase them, create them, plan them, anticipate them, and reminisce about them. If it calls or excites you (and it's safe enough), do more of it! If it makes your heart sing, sing along.

We need to jump off our hedonic treadmills, think and break outside the boxes, get out of and *expand* our comfort zones!

Having peak experiences, experiencing awe, engaging in growth, finding new hobbies, exploring new places, meeting new people, learning new skills, playing new games, etc. are all happiness builders. In addition to comfort and security, we need excitement. In the words of Helen Keller, "life is either a daring adventure or nothing at all."

32.
Surround yourself with happiness

Happiness should be all around you.

Paint your walls yellow. Put out photos that make you happy. Put something enjoyable on your computer, tablet, and phone home screens. Be around people who make you smile. Do fun activities. Expose yourself to art that makes you feel good. Read books that make you think positively. Listen to upbeat music. Watch funny videos and movies. Browse happiness quotes. Be with cheerful people.

Bring more happiness into your life by having it around and noticing it. Make your world a happiness bubble!

33.

Have high hopes, but low expectations

Although it is good to have high hopes to aspire toward in the future, high expectations typically lead to disappointment and, therefore, unhappiness.

Having low expectations—if you have to have expectations at all—means that our expectations will either be met or exceeded, leading to the satisfaction of achievement rather than the dissatisfaction of disappointment. It has been said that expectations are premeditated disappointments. If you don't want to get disappointed, professional hippie Stephen Gaskin recommends to not get appointed in the first place.

Marcus Aurelius took this further by recommending that we start each day expecting the worst: "say to yourself in the early morning: I shall meet today ungrateful, violent, treacherous, envious, uncharitable people." After doing that, everything might wind up better than expected, which leads to happier outcomes!

34.
Get things done

Getting necessary tasks accomplished and getting organized is good for both productivity and happiness.

Gretchen Rubin's one-minute rule from her *Happiness Project* suggests that you do any task that can be finished in about one minute—I personally think about 5 or so minutes is a better standard—and then cross it off your list and congratulate yourself for doing it.

Get things done and enjoy how it feels!

35.

Savor the flavor

When something good happens, no matter how small or trivial, slow down, take it in, appreciate it, give it its due, comment on it, and, ideally, share the good with someone else. That is how we savor things: paying attention, acknowledging, and respecting them. Indeed, we savor by finding, recognizing, and remembering the miraculous in the mundane.

As an exercise to strengthen your happiness muscle, step out of the moment of enjoyment and notice that you are enjoying something. Tell yourself something positive about what you are enjoying and how you are feeling, give it respect and appreciate it, express gratitude for it, note that it is an awesome experience, and try to tell someone else about how wonderful it is. Doing this savoring exercise is associated with greater happiness.

As another exercise, you can also recall positive experiences you have had in the past, conjure them for several minutes into their own mental movie. Think about the characters, location, lighting, feelings, etc., and do this with the same or other memories every day.

By savoring good times, we relive them and hang on to them longer, thus elongating our happiness.

36.

Break dependencies, addictions, and bad habits

Being dependent on *anything*—caffeine, nicotine, alcohol, drugs, screens, sugar, certain foods or drinks, brands, routines, certain people, TV, sports teams, social media, video games, porn, shopping, debt, weather, habits, a certain chair, a particular time of the day, winning, quietude, etc.—restricts your freedom and constrains your happiness, despite whatever benefits they may seem to generate. It is OK to enjoy or despise these types of things, but it is not good for our happiness to be addicted to and dependent on our habits.

Ozan Varol, author of *Think Like a Rocket Scientist*, discovered that "if you're not careful, your routines and habits can become traps." Varol continued: "if you can't adapt—if you've trained yourself to perform only under the perfect conditions—you'll stagnate when the universe delivers you an unexpected hand (and the universe has a way of delivering unexpected hands)." Any dependencies or addictions you have can limit your cognitive, emotional, and physical freedom. Liberate yourself for maximum potential!

There are various phenomena that seem to recur for most of us, often causing distress, anger, frustration, fear, resentment, annoyance, self-doubt, self-criticism, and so on. Some of these include traffic, certain weather, loud noises, rude people, relationship difficulties, family issues, long lines, unpleasant memories, random distractions, disrespect, and so on. Each of these seem to increase stress, anxiety, and unhappiness for many of us.

Buddha taught that suffering exists, but also that we can transcend it. Figuring out how to bar these phenomena from triggerring you will bring you peace, equanimity, and joy. All gain, no loss, but not necessarily easy. In Buddhism, there are two metaphorical arrows. The first one is the external stimulus. The second arrow is how we react to the first one. The self-inflicted second arrow is often at least as dangerous as the first.

It is not really those various issues I mentioned above, or any other external things, that are the problem: how we react to them is. Ultimately it is *us*, not them.

Swami Satchidananda, the founder of Integral Yoga, teaches us that "if you are in control of yourself, nobody can provoke you." Johann Wolfgang Von Goethe put it this way: "they who are plenteously provided for from within, need but little from without."

37.
Get out in nature

Nature is natural medicine that connects us with the world around us: basking in sunlight, feeling a soft breeze, breathing fresh air, breathing in more oxygen, and standing in awe of our majestic surroundings. Being in nature can reduce stress, anxiety, and other forms of negative thinking, leading to more happiness. Take time to notice whatever nature is around you, whether it is trees, a forest, an ocean, urban green space, a park, some water, stargazing, a flower, a bird, a bee, or even a single leaf.

"I felt my lungs inflate with the onrush of scenery—air, mountains, trees, people," poet and novelist Sylvia Plath mused. "I thought, 'this is what it is to be happy.'" Even short stints with the natural world, as little as 10–20 minutes, can improve mood and reduce anxiety. Being outdoors in the sunshine is also correlated with happiness. Even watching nature videos can help, especially when you cannot physically get out in nature or are stuck in an urban metropolis.

38.
Buy your way out of drudgery

If you do not enjoy cleaning your home or doing laundry, pay someone else to do it and free up time for yourself. You will be creating a paid job for someone who needs it while also ridding yourself of an unpleasant task, thereby increasing your happiness. You can also try to barter and exchange goods and services. In addition to outsourcing work you do not want to do, other forms of time affluence make us richer in happiness. In terms of happiness, time is more valuable than money.

39.
Avoid toxins

Toxins are toxic, and toxic things are poisonous.

Avoid toxic chemicals, foods, workplaces, people, relationships, consumption, habits, activities, stress, anger, news, social media, music, TV, thoughts, language, and behaviors.

All of these are bad for our health and happiness. Live clean!

40.
Get enough sleep…

Regularly getting enough sleep—at least 7 hours per night—is vitally important for your brain and body to rejuvenate.

Research shows that sleep is inextricably linked to our happiness, due to its relationships to stress, levels of depression, heart disease, diabetes, pain, concentration, emotion regulation, and so on.

Sleep your way to a happier you.

41.
Can you smell the happiness?

Whether it is smelling the flowers, smelling certain essential oils, or smelling something else you enjoy—vanilla, coconut, berries, rosemary, etc.—these odors can activate the ancient part of our brain, awaken our senses, and make us happier.

Use aromatherapy to bolster yourself.

42.
Consider wabi-sabi

Wabi-sabi is the Japanese art and philosophy of imperfection and impermanence.

Recognizing that no one is perfect, and that no one has to be, can free us up to be happy with who and what we are, while also appreciating others for who and what *they* are. Wabi-sabi encourages us to appreciate, embrace, and enjoy the beauty of imperfections, both ours and others', recognizing that nothing is forever.

Embracing imperfection can also liberate us by allowing us to start new things—writing, drawing, building, cooking, inventing, speaking up, playing, practicing, etc.—without worrying if we are expert enough to do so.

We do not have to be, nor can we ever be, perfect because we are human. We can and should sidestep the debilitating concept of perfectionism so we can enjoy the imperfections of the world. Including our own.

43.
Reconsider your bucket

It can be fun to make and have a bucket list, but it can also weigh us down and disappoint us. Although there is much we might like to read, try, taste, see, and do, there is nothing that we must do.

Ignore the imperative "must-do," "must-have," "must-go," "must-see," "must-try," and so on, unless you desire it. Whatever it is, it is *not* required or mandatory.

Your list is complete and accomplished simply by being alive and being your best you.

44.

Be Stoic

Accept whatever comes and make peace with what does not, regardless of how you feel about them. Nearly two thousand years ago, Stoic philosopher Epictetus encouraged us to recognize the fact that everything is temporary and that all things have their season, literally and figuratively. Everything—whether we want it, love it, or not—is fragile and fleeting. We need to realize that and react accordingly.

Feeling grief over the loss of someone or something is, to Epictetus, like "wishing for a fig in winter" or rain in the dry season. Doing so will only bring unhappiness, as we cannot have what we cannot have, no matter how much we might want it. We cannot control what we cannot control. Enjoy figs in fig season, rain in the rainy season, and enjoy other things and people in *their* seasons.

"The only thing you can really control," Bassam Tarazi says, "is how you react to things out of your control." Realizing that we need not and indeed cannot control what and how others think, say, or do, our only job is to control and conquer ourselves.

We can see versions of the philosophy of Stoicism in Buddhism, Taoism, Ecclesiastes, pragmatism, the Japanese concept of *ukeireru* (acceptance), Reinhold Niebuhr's Serenity Prayer, and elsewhere, all of which can help us with happiness by making peace with reality.

45.
Learn

Learning can help us become happier.

Listen to happiness podcasts and speeches. Watch happiness videos and documentaries. Read happiness books and articles. Take happiness courses online or off, as well as other genres you enjoy. Practice what you learn. Share your knowledge with others.

Teaching others is also a great way to learn.

46.
Be creative

Use your imagination and let it infuse your mind and the world.

Draw, paint, collage, sculpt, craft, journal, photograph, build, sew, knit, crochet, sing, play, dance, write, etc.

There are mental health and happiness benefits of making even mediocre art, regardless of form. If necessary, let *meh* be your medicine, as long as you enjoy it!

47.

Be your own cheerleader

We need to transform our inner critics and inner cops, who harass and abuse us, into inner coaches, inner cheerleaders, and inner best friends—all of which compassionately guide, support, and sustain us.

In a form of emotional jujitsu, use the power of your internal ferocious harshness against itself to transform it into a fierce instrument of self-love, self-care, self-protection, and self-promotion. That way, you can be your best, happiest, and most successful self. As Voltaire wrote, "we must cultivate our garden."

Cheers to you!

48.
WOOP it up!

WOOP is an acronym to help us remember an effective technique developed by Gabriele Oettingen. WOOP reminds us to think about our **W**ish, imagine the best **O**utcome, consider the **O**bstacles, then create a specific if/then **P**lan to help us succeed over the difficulties involved. As a result, our mental map is positively altered. Making a specific plan, inspired by our wish and hope for the best outcome, is key to having our wishes come true.

Oettingen says "the solution isn't to do away with dreaming and positive thinking. Rather, it's making the most of our fantasies by brushing them up against the very thing most of us are taught to ignore or diminish: the obstacles that stand in our way." When we plan to overcome our obstacles, accomplish our goals, and are more successful in our lives, we can be happier.

49.
FOMO → JOMO

Transform the fear of missing out (FOMO) into the *joy* of missing out (JOMO).

We will always miss out on some things, indeed many things, and that's OK. It might even be more than OK.

Embrace the silver linings of life, enjoy the "road not taken," emphasize the positives you are experiencing, focus on and appreciate what you have in the real world instead of what you imagine in the abstract. Be glad you are doing what you are doing at any given time instead of imagining or doing something else. It might make all the difference.

50.
Precrastinate

Precrastination is about shifting *when* we do whatever it is we have to do from later to sooner. Precrastination provides the same benefit as procrastination—free time without effort or work—but does so without as much stress.

Instead of procrastinating and putting off the work for another time, thereby enjoying what seems like free time, precrastination is accomplishing the work early and then enjoying the truly free time afterward without having the burden of our task still hanging over us. Precrastination is about shifting how and when you do tasks to increase your happiness. You control the task and time instead of letting them control you.

51.
Heal yourself

You can heal yourself, though you may need help doing so.

Engage in journaling or writing a diary, see a therapist, practice cognitive-behavioral therapy (CBT) techniques, join a support group, go on a retreat or to a spa, try forest bathing, meditate, inhale healing and exhale trauma, look deep within yourself and excise the pains of the past, forgive yourself and others, or do *whatever* it takes to make yourself whole and happy again.

Your pain and your trauma—your past—do *not* need to define or constrain you or make you unhappy.

The more you heal, the more you will be happy in the present and future.

52.

Interrupt good things

Good things are of course good, but they can be even better for us when they last longer in our lives. Interrupt good experiences to make them last longer and become more experiential. This will allow you more fully appreciate them as the good things that they are.

Take a break from doing what you enjoy and then get back to it later.

The longer we make good experiences last, and the more we revel in them as novel instead of commonplace, the more we experience them and the happier they tend to make us.

53.
Smoosh bad things together

In contrast to interrupting good things, smooshing bad things together to get them over with in one fell swoop also leads to happiness. Combining multiple bad things into one task or concurrent tasks means that, overall, we will spend less time, less thought, and less energy invested in bad things.

Our brains can't actually multi-task, but we can try to get as close as possible by setting aside one time period to tackle the tasks we most dislike and work through them until we finish. Procrastination is an understandable reaction to unpleasant tasks but stalling and putting them off just results in more time thinking about them and thus being weighed down. This will pollute times when you could otherwise be happy.

Try not to stretch out the time spent on unpleasant experiences, whether it is one task or a bunch. Just get it over with and be done with them. When we spend less time on bad things, we have more time, more energy, more brain power, and more opportunity for happiness.

54.
Gardening

From sowing to reaping, planting to harvesting, and much tending in between, there is a lot to be said about the benefits of gardening.

The slow pace, literally being grounded with the Earth, being out in the sun and fresh air, growing food, herbs, and/or flowers…all are pleasurable activities that can boost your happiness.

Subsequently having delicious food and beautiful flowers to enjoy without having to buy them is an added boost to happiness. Enjoy the process and reap the benefits to your physical and emotional wellbeing. You will revel in the joy of accomplishment and the unbeatable deliciousness of what you have grown!

When you grow a garden, you also grow yourself and grow your happiness.

55.
STOP

Jon Kabat-Zinn created the STOP technique to snap us out of mindless reaction and into mindful reflection. STOP is an acronym for Stop being on autopilot, Take a breath or two, Observe what's going on inside and out, then Proceed in a more conscious, mindful way.

STOPping is a good way to reboot and restart. Think of it like a buffer zone, insulaltion, a shock absorber, or a circuit breaker. When alone or in a safe space, some people like to yell STOP! Whenever and wherever you do it, STOP so you can more positively and productively restart.

Another similar yet different technique is RAIN, originally coined by Michele McDonald. In the words of Tara Brach, RAIN is a useful acronym to Recognize what is going on, Allow the experience to be there as it is, Investigate it with kindness, and have Natural loving awareness—which comes from not identifying with the experience. Some people suggest the N should be for Nurture.

56.
Take a placebo

Placebos are some of the world's most powerful medicines because they aren't medicine; they harness the power of *you*!

Placebos are powerful because the approximately three pounds of gray mush in our heads are the most sophisticated and amazing computers in the world. If you believe it, you can do and be it. Use your placebo mind and expect to be happier.

If it helps to take a little sugar pill to believe in yourself, by all means go for it!

57.
Solve it

Instead of simply complaining about problems—or viewing them as fate, bad luck, inevitable, deserved, imposed, oppressive, or otherwise giving in to the problems—become a solutionary.

Solutionaries seek comprehensive solutions that address root causes instead of only focusing on the problems or the symptoms of the problems themselves. Black feminist theorist Audre Lorde once said, "we are not responsible for our oppression, but we must be responsible for our own liberation." So, complain if you must, but you must take action to fix what you are complaining about.

Solutionaries take action and get things done for positive change.

58.
Carpe Diem

We are more likely to regret what we don't do instead of what we actually do—and getting new and more experiences is linked to happiness. Carpe diem is the Latin phrase for "seize the day," meaning that you should "enjoy yourself while you have the chance."

In *Dead Poets Society*, Robin Williams' character bluntly tells his students that "we are food for worms." Likewise, the Latin phrases *sic transit gloria mundi* (thus passes worldly glory) and *memento mori* (remember that you will die) and the Persian and Jewish adage "this too shall pass" remind us that time is fleeting. We should make the most of it while we can.

As an exercise, some people picture themselves far in the future, or as old and infirm, or on their deathbed, or even as dead—often called prospective retrospection—and they use that perspective to not waste the time they have by seizing the good opportunities whenever they arise.

Make the day yours and make it a great day!

59.

As if

This is *not* meant in the classic *Clueless* Cher Horowitz way of saying no way.

You can act *as if* you are happy, *as if* you are an extrovert, as if you are motivated, passionate, ready for anything. Your brain cannot tell the difference. "Fake it until you make it" is popular with cognitive-behavioral therapy (CBT) approaches and has been used in 12-step programs, such as Alcoholics Anonymous, for decades.

As an exercise, try looking in the mirror and say "action," *as if* you are a happy character ready for a positive performance. It is fine to pretend, to play a role, to be a character, to step outside of yourself, *as if* you are someone who is happier. And if you do, you just might become that happier person.

60.
Don't be boring

Fear is boring, Unhappiness is boring.

Elizabeth Gilbert, author of *Eat, Pray, Love*, recalls in *Big Magic* that "I somehow figured out that my fear had no variety to it, no depth, no substance, no texture. I noticed that my fear never changed, never delighted, never offered a surprise twist or an unexpected ending." Instead, Gilbert realizes, "we must have the stubbornness to accept our gladness in the ruthless furnace of this world."

Gilbert audaciously asks: "do you have the courage to bring forth the treasures that are hidden within you?"

Gilbert continues: "surely something wonderful is sheltered inside you. I say this with all confidence, because I happen to believe we are all walking repositories of buried treasure. I believe this is one of the oldest and most generous tricks the universe plays on us human beings, both for its own amusement and for ours: The universe buries strange jewels deep within us all, and then stands back to see if we can find them. The hunt to uncover those jewels—that's creative living. The courage to go on that hunt in the first place—that's what separates a mundane existence from a more enchanted one. The often surprising results of that hunt—that's what I call Big Magic."

It is time to ditch the boring and embrace the magic!

61.
Satisfice

Satisficing is about accepting a satisfactory option, instead of seeking to maximize your options.

Trying to maximize what we get increases our likelihood of being disappointed, while satisficing gets us what we like. Sometimes good enough is the best option.

We can't always get what we want, as the Rolling Stones suggested, but we can often get what we need.

62.
Change your situation

Sometimes we need to change our situation to be better able to change our mind and mood. When necessary, avoid triggering situations, get away from vampires who suck your life force, exit yourself from overwhelming negativity.

We can, for example, step away from a person or place, leave a room and enter another, pause and take a few deep breaths, switch activities, change the subject, check our phone, take a walk, engage in distraction, give ourselves a time out, whatever it takes to extricate ourselves from emotionally dangerous or otherwise overly fraught situations.

Although this does not necessarily get at the root of an issue, treating symptoms can also be worthwhile, giving us the time and space to deal with the larger issues.

63.
Realize

Realize that we could not exist in this time and in this place, with this level of understanding and reading these very words, if it were not for the forming of this universe: this level of cosmic expansion; this amount of gravity; the creation of this nearby star we call the sun; this amount of heat; this amount of atmosphere; this amount of carbon, nitrogen, hydrogen, and oxygen; this amount of microflora and microfauna; this type, structure, and amount of DNA, chromosomes, and genes; this level of evolution; this lineage that allowed every ancestor of ours since the very beginning of life on Earth to live at least as long as their time of reproduction; this level of childcare; this level of innovation, education, language, and culture; this level of cooperation and competition; and the kindness of others.

These phenomena are so highly unlikely, almost impossible, yet here we are. Realizing all this, we should smile and be happy.

64.

Don't do anything

The Taoist concept of *wu-wei*, developed in China about two and half millennia ago, is the philosophy of non-action, especially in the sense of not forcing anything to happen. If there is any action at all, it is a spontaneous and effortless action—like the flow of water, the blowing of the breeze, or the growing of a tree.

The *Tao Te Ching* philosophically relates: "in the pursuit of learning, every day something is acquired.

In the pursuit of Tao, every day something is dropped.

Less and less is done

Until non-action is achieved.

When nothing is done, nothing is left undone.

The world is ruled by letting things take their course.

It cannot be ruled by interfering."

According to *The Complete Idiot's Guide to Taoism*, "*Wu-wei* means responding completely, authentically, and spontaneously to the emerging circumstances of one's environment— without employing what some Zen teachers call a 'grasping idea' or 'monkey mind.'"

Just like nature itself, take life as it comes. Don't do; just be. It is more than enough. Simply enjoy what ensues.

65.
Practice lovingkindness

Lovingkindness has a long history in many different cultures. It is called *metta* in Hinduism, Jainism, and Buddhism; *jampa* in Tibetan Buddhism; *chesed* in Judaism; and *agape* in Christianity.

Lovingkindness is a form of active benevolence, deeply caring for the wellbeing of others. Regardless of whether it benefits others, it definitely does benefit those who practice it in terms of health and happiness. It feels good to be loving and kind, and the rewards for doing so are instantaneous but also long lasting.

Jack Kerouac suggested to "practice kindness all day to everybody and you will realize you're already in heaven now."

66.
Set small goals

Set at least one small goal to make your life better that you can definitely accomplish each day—1 minute of meditation, 5 minutes of exercise, or listing 3 things you are grateful for. Then, accomplish it and celebrate that you accomplished it. Yay!

Something does not have to be a big deal to have a big impact. As Iris Murdoch says, "one of the secrets of a happy life is continuous small treats."

67.
Minimize taking things for granted

Don't take things for granted.

It is easy to get used to things, to grow accustomed, to habituate ourselves. When we get used to things and take them for granted, we no longer derive as much pleasure from them.

In contrast, when we see them as new, special, rare, not guaranteed, or a miracle, we begin to appreciate them again and they can make us happier. That's what blessings are all about!

68.
Re-experience the good times

Taking time to remember, reminisce, and re-experience the good times will bring more happiness back to your life—even more so when you share the stories, photos, or videos with others.

"When I'm feeling sad,
I simply remember my favorite things,
And then I don't feel so bad." ♫

69.
Be resilient

There will *always* be stressors, but that does not necessarily mean we have to get stressed out.

In the face of stress, threat, or crisis, it is worst to break, bad to weaken, good to resist, and great to be resilient. Many refer to this as grit, which allows us to be nimble and agile when necessary. Even better is to be anti-fragile, becoming stronger, and maybe happier, in response to difficulties.

Charles Darwin famously observed that "it is not the strongest of the species that survives, nor the most intelligent that survives. It is the one that is most adaptable to change." Change is the only constant.

70.
Are you curious?

Curiosity is a key to happiness because it opens us up to the world, keeps us engaged and active, introduces new thoughts and information, and provides entertainment and meaning in our lives.

Pursue things with passion, whatever they are, including your own thoughts and emotions!

And as oral historian Studs Terkel famously declared, "curiosity never killed *this* cat."

71.

Disbelieve

Not everything is the real deal, so don't believe everything you think and feel. It may not be an accurate representation of reality.

We *have* thoughts and feelings, but we are not our thoughts and feelings. They are subjective and subject to error. Both Pema Chödrön and Eckhart Tolle suggested that "you are the sky" and everything else—including our thoughts and feelings—is just the clouds and the weather that come and go, blowing this way and that.

Interrogate what you think and feel. Ask and answer why you think and feel that way, going as deep as you can to the root of the issue. This is one technique to achieve "flow consciousness." In any event, whatever it is, it is not forever and it will pass.

72.
Breathe

Breathe in, breathe out.

Take some deep breaths, especially by letting your exhales be longer than your inhales.

There may not be anything magical about focusing on our breathing, as opposed to anything else, but our breath is always accessible and rhythmically there for us. It brings us back to who we are and what we all naturally do as animals.

There are many different types and techniques of breathing. Being conscious of your breath and practicing certain breathing techniques can bring peace, wisdom, and happiness.

Breathe in, breathe out. Repeat as necessary.

73.
Make peace

Make peace with whoever or whatever bothers you, even if you are trying to change it. The world—including everyone and everything in it—is what it is, just as we are what we are.

Reality is a durable illusion. The less we fight it, the happier we will be. "How we orient ourselves to our suffering," Maria Popova suggests, "may be the single most significant predictor of our happiness, wellbeing, and capacity for joy."

Healthy resignation, as Rick Hanson calls it, is not about quitting nor the same as surrendering. This type of resignation, a healthy resignation, is simply recognizing what is and making peace with the reality of it, regardless of how one might feel about it.

There are various versions of Reinhold Niebuhr's Serenity Prayer, written in 1932-33, which originally stated: "give us courage to change what must be altered, serenity to accept what cannot be helped, and the insight to know the one from the other."

74.

Be present

The past and future are interesting and powerful concepts, but there is really only an endless series of nows and presents. These are gifts, if we properly accept them.

The past is always gone, the future never arrives, and the present is all we have. It is always right now. Now.

Everything we think, we remember from the past. Everything we imagine about the future is completely contained in the omnipresent and eternal now. It is always now. Now. Now. Now. Eternally now.

We need to be present to the present for happier and optimal results.

75.

Balance

Find balance in your thoughts and activities, alone time and relationships, words and actions, work and play, being home and away, your journey and destination.

Every time you get too out of balance—which is normal and inevitable—gently guide yourself back.

Our middle path is our happy path.

76.
THINK

Before you communicate, pause to THINK.

Check whether what you are thinking, saying, or writing is **T**houghtful, **H**elpful, **I**ntelligent, **N**ecessary, and **K**ind.

Delete the thoughtless negativity out of your life and relationships. Doing so will reduce drama, misunderstandings, and arguments, which will result in a happier life.

THINK happiness!

77.

Meet and greet

Whenever fear, pain, anger, resentment, or whatever else arises to interfere with your happiness, meet that feeling, perhaps as a fictional character. Recognize it, greet it, even get to know it and understand it a bit. Ideally empathize and make peace with it.

When you are ready, let it go and send it on its way so it can continue its journey as you happily continue yours.

78.
Visit a waterfall

Visiting a waterfall allows you to be in nature, experience awe, and bask in the negative ions that spray into the air that are connected with higher energy and positive moods. It is also just a fun, new experience.

As an alternative, seek out other bodies of water—the ocean, a river, even a lake. Also consider virtual waterfall tours online.

79.
Identify what moves you

Identify what you care most about, what *really* matters to you, where your passion lays, and what brings your senses to life.

Focus on your strengths and talents, then pursue those things with vigor.

Give yourself permission and opportunity to live your best and most passionate life. When we live more in our strengths, we live more in our happiness.

80.
Disoblige

We are not as obliged to other people's demands as we sometimes imagine.

Of course there are things we must do, but sometimes we come to believe that our options are requirements. When someone calls us, we are not required to check or answer our phone whether we know who is calling or not. It is not an obligation that we owe anyone else. Indeed, we need to use our tools, not have them, and others, use us.

To be obliged is to be bound to others. To disoblige is to act contrary to the whims or convenience of another.

Another way to think about this phenomenon is at *The Crossroads of Should and Must*, a wise book written by Elle Luna. "Should is how other people want us to live our lives," Luna writes, while "choosing Must is the greatest thing we can do with our lives."

When we create, find, and follow our passions, instead of binding ourselves to other people's dictates, we can live a more authentic, more satisfying, more joyful life.

As we decrease obligations, we increase happiness.

81.
Snap out of it

Some people snap out of negative thinking, compulsive behaviors, or other addictions by snapping a rubber band around their wrist. Instead of a rubber band, it could also be a symbolic string or bracelet. Some people keep a small object in their pocket, like a pebble or a bead, as something they could touch for security and grounding.

Even less physical, we can simply say "snap" or "delete" to delete whatever thoughts or feelings we no longer need or want at the moment.

82.
What if?

Instead of the seemingly infinite negative "what ifs" that people tend to engage with, try consciously flipping them to positive "what ifs?"

What if everything goes great? What if we excel? What if things work out well? What if the process is smooth? What if we are happy?

83.
WWAHPD?

When you are tired of being unhappy and want to be happy, try asking yourself a simple question: what would a happy person do (WWAHPD)?

Just asking that question can break us out of our cognitive and emotional cycle, thereby giving us the space and opportunity to consciously choose a happier path for ourselves.

Then, we can answer the question and actually *do* it—even if it is not what we would ordinarily do. It's OK to do something different and it's great to be happy!

84.
Count your blessings

When we count our blessings, we are being more aware—noticing, recognizing, and remembering them. Then, we are in a better position to appreciate the all the good things in life.

Some people keep a blessings jar or journal to explicitly catalog *at least* one good thing each day, regardless of whatever else may have happened. Blessings are blessings.

Whether religiously or secularly, we have all been blessed in many ways. We can always go to our jar or journal and pluck out some blessings to read and remember when necessary.

85.
Admit it

When you are not happy—stressed, scared, anxious, angry, offended, in pain, etc.—admit it.

It is better to be upfront and honest with ourselves and others. Trying to hide it rarely works and never makes it go away. Recognize it, label it, respect it, allow yourself to feel and understand it, congratulate yourself on admitting it, and allow yourself to move on and get back to happiness.

Some people recommend welcoming it to sit and have tea with you. Spend some time with it before sending it along on its way.

Dan Brook, PhD

86.
Let it go, let it flow

We do not have to carry unnecessary burdens that weigh us down, slow us down, tear us down, and tire us out. We can let it go and leave it there.

Whatever is weighing you down or holding you back does not have to do so. Whether you say, "so what?," "whatever," or "it is what it is," find your way to let it go!

You have the power to choose what to let go and when.

Ajahn Chah, a Thai monk, said, "if you let go a little, you'll have a little peace. If you let go a lot, you'll have a lot of peace. If you let go completely, you'll be completely peaceful."

It might be grudges, regrets, abuse, addiction, negativity, meanness, insensitivity, self-doubt, worries, bad feelings, past pain, failed relationships, resentment, trauma, loss, fear, old habits, dependence, or whatever else. You do not have to carry it with you anymore.

Let it go, let it flow, leave it in the past, and free yourself from the burden. Let yourself be free and happy.

87.
Align yourself

Our culture does not always encourage consistency, therefore many of us are unaligned, fragmented, and polarized. At the same time, consistency and integrity can make us happier because we can be more authentic and whole beings.

"Happiness," according to Mahatma Gandhi, "is when what you think, what you say, and what you do are in harmony." Align yourself by being more consistent in thought, speech, and action.

88.
Emulate those who inspire you

We need not and cannot be other people, just as no one else can be you. However, we can emulate the good qualities of those people we admire and look up to.

We can be kind like one person, thoughtful like another, generous like someone else, and so on.

By incorporating some good qualities from other people who we admire, we can become better and happier people ourselves—all while becoming the person who other people admire and look up to.

89.
Babies

Most babies are undeniably cute. We can conjure them, real or imagined, whenever we want or need to.

Sixteenth-century Jewish mystic Rabbi Moses Cordovero suggested seeing everyone in the "innocence of their infancy," which can be especially helpful during stressful and strifeful times.

You can also do this with yourself. You, too, were once a cute little baby, completely innocent.

90.
Say yes!

Saying "yes!" to as many opportunities as possible will bring more experiences, excitement, and fun into your life.

Improv master Patricia Ryan Madson suggests that "when the answer to all questions is yes, you enter a new world, a world of action, possibility, and adventure."

There is more than enough negativity, pessimism, cynicism, and fear in the world. We don't need to add more.

Experiment with saying yes to people, questions, offers, and opportunities. By saying yes—with certain exceptions, of course—we are more likely to see the positive, more likely to have good experiences, and more likely to become a "can-do" person. Therefore, we're more likely to enjoy life.

91.
Challenge yourself

When worry or anxiety heightens, depression starts creeping in, and fear starts to rear, challenge yourself about your perceptions and the lenses through which you see the world.

In what ways might your perceptions not be accurate? How can you see through other lenses?

Whether you try a clearer lens or rose-tinted ones, try a different perspective to acquire a different and happier attitude.

92.
Talk to strangers

Everybody has stories within them, and many of them are fascinating!

We don't talk to strangers often enough, ignoring each other as we stay within our individualistic silos and little bubbles. We are a social species; we need each other.

Some of us avoid strangers because we are scared, don't want to bother people, don't want to get involved, don't know how to start or what to say, were told not to, etc.

Research shows that people don't mind being bothered as much as we expect, and we tend to enjoy the interactions more than we expect ourselves.

You could talk about anything, but it is also interesting to ask people about their best day, their most enjoyable experience, or their favorite something. Encourage them by saying "tell me more."

93.
Play

Play is normal, natural, universal, and fun!

Thai culture has the philosophy of *sanuk*, which is to make any activity fun in some way—even if it is not inherently so.

Whether it is normal or weird, business or pleasure, boring or exciting, mundane or amazing, it's fun to be silly and playful. When we play, we are more likely to be happy.

Many adults no longer play, so we have to reclaim this precious activity from the kids—or just join them!

94.
Get a pet

Although it varies by person and animal, having a pet can be a major happiness boost.

The social bonding, attention, cuddling, playing, and more that people and their pets provide for each other can increase happiness for all involved.

Cats and dogs are the most popular pets, but there are many other possibilities. My family had a succession of rats while my son was growing up. Each rat was sweet, social, friendly, funny, clean, and loving animals. They enriched our lives as we tried to enrich theirs, and we remember them fondly.

95.
Reframe

"When you change the way you look at things," Wayne Dyer reveals, "the things you look at change."

Elizabeth Scott says "cognitive distortions, or patterns of faulty thinking, can impact our thoughts, behaviors, and experience of stress," but that "a little cognitive restructuring can bring significant change."

Whether it is mental exercises, cognitive-behavioral therapy (CBT), cognitive reappraisal, or some other method, reframing or rechanneling your thoughts into more realistic or positive directions can help tremendously. That's positive neuroplasticity!

Marcus Aurelius observed over 1900 years ago that "the happiness of your life depends upon the quality of your thoughts."

The great science fiction writer Ursula K. Le Guin remarked that "suffering is a misunderstanding." Attitude is everything.

One simple trick is to just find life amusing, regardless of what is going on, and to be amused by the world's inherent absurdity and ridiculousness—even enjoy it!—instead of feeling frustrated, annoyed, worried, anxious, fearful, guilty, upset, angry, resentful, insulted, disrespected, envious, jealous, bored, confused, etc.

Try considering whatever happens as performance art or public theatre: something that is happening in front of you, yet not happening *to* you. Another trick is to feel excited instead of anxious, challenged instead of blocked, appreciative instead of desirous, grateful instead of dissed.

Anything and everything can be a teacher, source of entertainment, or both.

Henry Ford remarked that "if you think you can do a thing or think you can't do a thing, you're right." Similarly, Wayne Dyer advised "if you believe it will work out, you'll see opportunities; if you believe that it won't, you'll see obstacles."

Get some perspective and try to see the bigger picture. Imagine a difficult situation or negative feeling as far away, creating emotional distance from it.

We cannot control other people and most phenomena; most things will not matter in the future. Most things seem small and less significant from far enough or long enough away. We only have one wild and precious life to live.

We have power over ourselves, including our thoughts, feelings, and emotions. You cannot control other people, or *any* external phenomena, but you have the power to control yourself. What other people think, say, and do is their business, their responsibility, and only represents them. How you react and what you think, say, and do is your business, your responsibility, and only represents you.

Remember, the more you find life funny, the more fun you will have!

96.
Visualize

Visualize a happy you. Picture yourself happy. What might you look like? Add details.

Like a form of meditation, use your imagination to visualize how you would look, feel, perhaps even sound and smell, etc. to be happy. Visualize yourself smiling, in a place that makes you happy, where you feel safe, secure, and content.

Visualize your best self, knowing that your best self is happy. Repeat this visualization technique whenever and wherever necessary.

97.

Biohack

Biohack your brain and body to increase your happiness.

Breathe deeply. Make your exhales longer than your inhales. Activate your vagus nerve. Consciously control the reptilian part of your brain. Manage your stress and emotions. Eat clean. Get enough sleep. Meditate. Practice gratitude. Visualize what you want. Decide you want to be happy. Release your dopamine, serotonin, oxytocin, and other happiness chemicals that your body and brain naturally produce, while minimizing the release of cortisol.

98.
Change the world

Minnesota Sen. Paul Wellstone famously said, "we all do better when we all do better." Creating more egalitarian societies, where people's needs are met, tends to increase happiness for the majority of people.

According to data collected by social scientists Richard Wilkinson and Kate Pickett in *The Spirit Level: Why Greater Equality Makes Societies Stronger*, "the correlations are terrifying in their clarity and consistency. To put it simply, the more unequal a society, the worse off most of its citizens were. This didn't just play out on one or two metrics. When compared with more equal societies with similar incomes, more unequal societies had worse infant mortality, worse educational scores, higher teen pregnancies, more [students] dropping out of high school, more drug abuse, more homicides, more mental illness, more people in prison, greater obesity, more health problems overall and shorter lives. [In contrast, in addition to having fewer of those social problems,] societies that were more equal showed higher innovation, greater use of environmental resources, and ... greater social mobility [as well as greater levels of well-being, trust, empathy, generosity, and support for foreign aid]."

Whether it is supporting Black Lives Matter, environmental sustainability, or any other social cause for good, it is also good for you.

99.
Enjoy the process

It is natural to want certain results, especially with wholesome desires, but the process it takes to get there is the longer, more important, more interesting, and more controllable portion of what we do.

The road itself is the destination.

Prioritizing process over product, effort over result, is a recipe for happiness. The hyphen between our birth date and death date is nearly our whole life, so enjoy your hyphen, so you can enjoy your life to the fullest.

100.
Use the proper tool

Every year, I bring students to Thailand for a special course I teach. As part of our day trekking in the countryside through villages and past rice paddies, we go bamboo rafting down a picturesque river in Chiang Mai province.

When we are going down the river, the bamboo raft is a great way to float and is essential for that particular journey. However, no matter how much we enjoy bamboo rafting—and we really do!—the bamboo raft is not only unessential while we are on land, but ridiculously heavy, cumbersome, and worse than useless.

Using appropriate tools for their proper purposes is a path of peace and happiness. When we do so, we can enjoy what we are doing and be more successful without any unnecessary drama, strife, and frustration.

101.
Be

If you want to skip all the other steps, you can still be happy. It is ultimately your choice!

Leo Tolstoy once simply said, "if you want to be happy, be."

Some people like to say that this is easier said than done. It is and isn't. It is actually as easy, or as difficult, or as possible or impossible, as you choose it to be.

If you decide you want to be happy, you will be happy. "Happiness is an attitude," and it takes about the same energy to be happy as to be sad, miserable, or angry. Regardless of the past, every *moment* is another opportunity for you to choose happiness and a joyful life.

Therapist, meditation leader, and author Rick Hanson suggests, "no matter what is happening in the world around us, no matter what situation we're stuck in, no matter how anguished we are for others, no matter how hopeless it seems and helpless we feel—we can always turn to joy, claim it, and welcome it."

We should remember, in the words of Guillaume Apollinaire, that "now and then it's good to pause in our pursuit of happiness and just be happy." Perhaps "there is no way to happiness," as Zen Master Thich Nhat Hanh says, "happiness is the way."

Or, as Eleanor Roosevelt advised, "happiness is not a goal... it's a by-product of a life well lived."

You are a human being, not a human doing, so just be—and be happy.

Want more?

Feel free to tweak and combine various methods, making them your own, to best suit your personality and desires for a more holistic, pleasurable, and meaningful approach to your happiness.

As psychologist Scott Barry Kaufman relates, "happy people tend to have a harmonious integration of meaning ('What I do matters to society'), pleasure ('I love to do things that excite my senses'), and engagement ('I am always very absorbed in what I do') in their lives."

If these possible paths are not enough for you, feel free to forge your own. Elizabeth Barrett Browning mused about "the wisdom of cheerfulness," while Colette wrote that happiness is "a way of being wise."

Rabbi Nachman of Breslov thought it a sin to be unhappy. Indeed, Rabbi Nachman believed that "joy is not merely incidental to your spiritual quest, it is vital ... Use every ploy you can think of to bring yourself to joy," adding "that you should even force yourself to be happy, if that's what it takes." Philosopher Albert Camus even suggested that happiness is a moral obligation, but that is for you to decide.

"Happiness is a spiritual path," Robert Holden realizes. "The more you learn about true happiness, the more you discover the truth of who you are, what is important, and what your life is really for."

In addition to the obvious benefit that being happier is better because you are happier, studies show that being happier is also healthier. Alexander Fanaroff, MD concludes that patients who "have better expectations for recovering have better long-term outcomes," because "happy thoughts may lead to better long-term health."

Just the thought of that makes me happy! I sincerely hope it helps you too.

Dan Brook, PhD

Dan Brook, PhD happily teaches sociology at San Jose State University, where he organizes the annual Hands on Thailand program. Dan has written Brook's Book, Eating the Earth (in various languages), and other freely available eBooks. He also wrote Sweet Nothings and edited the non-profit vegetarian cookbook Justice in the Kitchen. He welcomes communication from readers.

Testimonials

"For years, Renae has been bringing joy and cheer to The Lambs Club each and every weekend during the holiday season. Our entire team year after year waits with anticipation for the I SMILE in NY singers to arrive as it sets the tone for the whole month. We have had hundreds of diners enjoy these carolers and musical treasures. It would most certainly not be the holidays at The Lambs Club without Renae and I Smile in NY."

— **Margaret Zakarian**, President of Zakarian Hospitality LLC

"A visionary, a beautiful voice, a talented writer and a lover of Christmas; that's Renae Baker. Her masterful message is one of joy, peace, and blessed happiness. Renae is the messenger of the true Christmas Spirit that grows in our hearts throughout the entire year. This inspirational book is a gift, that you can open 365 days a year, and feel as good as the first time."

— **Nick Lawrence,** Radio talk show host of
"Straight Talk" and "Radio Voices", WEEU

"With her brilliant musical talents and joyful inner spirit I've seen Renae Baker brighten the lives of adults and children of all ages for many years. Renae has risen above and lived through many difficult times herself with courage, grace and laughter. She is an inspiration and a perfect guide to weather all the storms of our lives, especially those that seem the darkest around the holidays and show us all how to bring back the light and cheer."

— **Liz Bolick,** Miz Liz and Company

"It is so easy to 'miss' Christmas in the frantic New York City environment. Time goes by so fast and before you know it the Christmas season is over and often not appreciated. I get a great feeling of satisfaction when I walk through my building's lobby and observe people literally stopping in their tracks and taking a moment to listen to and maybe snap a photo of Renae and her carolers. It truly infuses a Christmas spirit into people's day and reminds them that Christmas is still here, alive and well."

— **Robert McKeown,** Director of Property Management, NYC

"Renae Baker has always been a positive and joyful energy in my life. Whether we are catching up or caroling. She truly embodies the Christmas spirit all year round."

— **Ian Knauer,** fellow caroler and Broadway actor

"Renae is the star on top of the tree. She radiates the light of Christmas Spirit every day and everywhere! It is always uplifting to be in her presence."

— **Babs Winn**, I SMILE caroler, singer/actress

"If you love Christmas carols, you are going to love this book even more. In her attempt to restore the faith that she had temporarily lost, Renae Baker takes us on her very personal journey of discovering the power of Christmas carols to revive your spirit all year long and not just at Christmas. In her attempt to really understand the essence of the lyrics of each carol she uncovers some amazing insights about the meaning of the words, the fascinating stories about the writing of the carols, and the stories of the miraculous effects the carols have created throughout history. This book is definitely chicken soup for my soul, and I know it will be for yours too."

—**Jack Canfield**, Cocreator of the Chicken Soup for the Soul® series including the *Chicken Soup for the Soul Christmas Treasury*

"Renae Baker is a national treasure. She has proven over and over that Christmas is not a time, nor a season, but a state of mind. She inspires throughout the year."

—**James "Jimmy" Spadola and Cliff Witmyer,**
Cliffhanger Productions, E. Rutherford, NJ

"Renae is a beacon of hope and true model of holiday spirit, unlocking joy in anyone who is lucky enough to be around her. She shines with Holiday Spirit all year long."

— **Susan Haefner**, fellow caroler, theatrical director and Broadway actress

"Renae Baker's years of experience in the industry as an acting coach combined with her wisdom, passion and human kindness make her an invaluable resource in the craft of acting. Her intuitive work with sense memory is a gift she has used to guide and mentor many actors to success on Broadway and in television and film. In this book she shows you how it can guide you to more holiday spirit. She is a well sought out coach for a reason — she is smart, trustworthy, reliable and a wonderful human."

— **Denise Simon**, Renowned Child Acting Expert & Coach and author of *Parenting in the Spotlight: How to raise a child star without screwing them up*

DEFEATING
SCROOGE

DEFEATING SCROOGE

How to Harness the Power of
Christmas Carols to Revive
Your Spirit Any Time of Year

Renae Baker
Dec. 1 2018

RENAE BAKER

Morway Media

Printed in the United States of America

First Printing: September 2018

ISBN: 978-1-7328525-0-1 (Paperback)

ISBN: 978-1-7328525-1-8 (Hardback)

Morway Media

New York, New York

Dedication

This book is dedicated to my carolers—from the first quartet in 1997, to each and every caroler who has added their voice to our merry troupe. Singing alongside you has taught me how joining voices together in service of others multiplies the joy we not only give but that we ourselves receive. You've helped me to learn to let go of worry; that I can rely on you to read a crowd and put them in the pocket of their holiday spirit; and that God always sends us just the caroler we need at precisely the right time. As we have learned scores of carol arrangements and performed in venues ranging from glorious stages to cozy living rooms by the fireside, your dedication, enthusiasm, spirit, and friendship have buoyed and enriched me more than I can adequately express. Hopefully you have seen the truest expressions of my appreciation in my eyes and heard it somewhere in the blend of our voices. Our caroling would ring hollow if it weren't for your spirit, but instead it rings like the bells Ebenezer heard on Christmas morning. And, so I say, "God bless us, every one!"

TABLE OF CONTENTS

ACKNOWLEDGMENTS

For years I looked for a coach to help me realize the completion of this book. It wasn't until I found Steve Harrison of Bradley Communications (or he found me?) that I was finally able to pull it together. With the help of him and his team, I was able to reach this goal even while enduring some of the most challenging trials of my life. Thank you, Steve, and to the coaches from your team who vigorously brainstormed with me and guided me to write the book I intended: Geoffrey, Martha, and Gail. Jack Canfield, your enthusiasm for this project and your charge to me to finish it right away gave me a big boost in my confidence to do so. I am humbled and amazed by the friends who spent great time and energy giving me feedback on my first draft: Sue, Andrea, Emily, Mark, Nick, Debra, Lisa, Wendy, and Bill, who has been my steadfast cheerleader as well. Charmaine, I thank you for your enthusiastic feedback and for a lifetime of being a trusted spiritual advisor to me. To Chanise, who helped bring some order to the chaotic times in my home—I would be buried under a heap of papers if it weren't for you! Thank you to my mother, Colleen, who planted the seed of Christmas joy in my heart and to my stepdad, Ed, who drove us around the United States and loved me as his own. To my book designer, Jerry. and my editor, Heidi, who gave me the leeway to take care of life in between progress on the book—thank you! To our music directors through the years, Joe and Dennis, who have guided us carolers to a beautiful sound, and Roo – who has not only led us, musically, but has been a shining example of what a caroler with great heart can be—how can I possibly thank you for giving us wings? To my children, Rozie and David, who gave me their version of high praise and encouragement in this venture, you are the sweetest carols in the songbook of my heart.

AUTHOR'S NOTE

My journey through the carols has wended me over winding roads and slipped me down rabbit holes where I am often surprised and delighted by discoveries I would not have made otherwise. One such eye-opener was the poem "Holidays" by Henry Wadsworth Longfellow.

It speaks of the hidden treasures, which are just what I set out to find during this quest, and it addresses the very idea that we are more likely to find them on unexpected days and during times of quiet reflection. The holiest of days can be, and often are, those that take us by surprise during what we expect to be ordinary days. This is something I have found to be true and plays a big part in my pursuit to revive my holiday spirit all through the year.

HOLIDAYS

The holiest of all holidays are those
Kept by ourselves in silence and apart;
The secret anniversaries of the heart,
When the full river of feeling overflows;—
The happy days unclouded to their close;
The sudden joys that out of darkness start
As flames from ashes; swift desires that dart
Like swallows singing down each wind that blows!
White as the gleam of a receding sail,
White as a cloud that floats and fades in air,
White as the whitest lily on a stream,
These tender memories are;— a Fairy Tale
Of some enchanted land we know not where,
But lovely as a landscape in a dream.

–Henry Wadsworth Longfellow, 1807–1882

INTRODUCTION

If you've picked up this book, you may be a lover of Christmas. You may be annoyed at Christmas. You may be someone who feels excluded from Christmas. You may be someone who rages against Christmas. No matter who you are, my guess is that you recognize that there is a palpable spirit of this season, and that, at some point or points in your life, you have felt the stinging absence of that spirit.

People who know me are often surprised to hear that I have experienced this crisis in my own life. Why are they surprised? Because not only do I have a reputation for loving Christmas and having Christmas spirit to spare, but, since 1997, I have been the founder and director of a company whose biggest offering is holiday carolers! My carolers refer to me as Mrs. Christmas, Queen of Christmas, and Christmas Boss. They tell me that my name has become synonymous with Christmas to them, which is the best compliment I can imagine receiving.

Christmas spirt has been a crown jewel of my life and has sustained me through some very tough times. And yet, one December, I was blind-sided with the realization that my spirit was missing in action! It was confusing. It was painful. As a professional caroler, I relied on my theatrical training and did something I never want to do again: I faked my way through the season.

During the holiday season, you (like me and so many others) may have the expectation of a warm and joyful experience. In fact, you might have, consciously or unconsciously, come to rely on this boost of joy and good feeling to recharge your spiritual or emotional battery every December. So, if you find that you feel like Scrooge—empty, with no warmth of the season lifting your spirits— then you are in a very painful place indeed.

I wrote this book to offer a balm and a tonic to heal this particular pain. I want to share my healing process, which will not only fascinate and entertain your conscious mind but can reset your spirit on a subconscious level.

A word to the wise: you cannot put a bandage on your spirit in December and expect a joyful experience. This repairing process is best begun earlier in the year.

My dis-spirited December led me to develop a process for nurturing and strengthening my spirit all through the year so that it would be there for me when I really needed it. It was an experiment, but I knew from the very first week that it was working. I already felt the excitement and the promise of my precious holiday spirit being revived!

A word to the wise: you cannot put a bandage on your spirit in December and expect a joyful experience. This repairing process is best begun earlier in the year.

After applying this process for several years now, I realized what I was actually doing and why it was working. When you stumble across a treasure like this, you *must* share it! I want you to feel the relief and the restoration of joy that I have been able to key into through this process.

Immediately following my spirit-less season,

when I first set out to rekindle my spirit, I felt like the captain of a ship trying to navigate across a dark ocean, without any stars for guidance. I was excited each step of the way, but finding my direction and charting a new course took time. I have since streamlined what I now call the Spirit Saver process and made this easy for you. You can even accomplish some of these daily steps while you're brushing your teeth in the morning.

In this book, I share my story and introduce you to the Spirit Saver process. In Chapters 3 to 11 you will learn some history and surprising facts about some of the best-known Christmas carols. I'll share some of the discoveries that I made about each carol that changed my perceptions of those carols, and how that information might apply to our lives today. I've included Spirit Saver workbook pages at the end of the book to help you start your own journey through the carols. You can download these pages and more by visiting www.ismileny.com.

My holiday spirit transcends the religious basis of Christmas and has been nothing less than a saving grace in my life. It has been a treasure that buoyed me through some of the worst of times, and helped me celebrate the good times to indescribable levels of joy. Without the aid of that spirit, God only knows where I'd be. Even in the years of my exploring and writing about this spirit, I have experienced heartbreak, trauma, and challenges like never before in my life.

I believe God set those trials in my way to make sure I knew some of the harder times that people go through so that I could relate to and have something meaningful to share with a wide range of people. And, you know what? This process—my journey through the carols—has helped me hold onto my determination to not only rise above that which threatens to harm me but also to continue seeking joy in my life. Over and over. I found this process to be a life-affirming help throughout each year, and because of the foundation the carols laid for me, my Decembers are joyful and triumphant!

Through this exploration, I have come to believe that carols are a key to healing our broken spirits. When our spirits are healed, there can be healing in our communities, and those healing waves can ripple through our country and even throughout our fractured world.

It feels as if our world is more divided than ever. People are shocked at the political views of friends, families, and people all over the world. They are losing faith in humanity. When the next holiday season rolls around, I expect that many people will be stunned to realize that their usual holiday spirit is missing. But the human spirit, in those moments of crisis, is stronger than we might believe. It is during the most trying times that we have a unique and wonderful opportunity to find out what our spirit is worth to us, what it's made of, and we are given the desire and determination to resuscitate it. My hope is that you read this book and start applying this process early enough in the year to take hold of those holiday reins and give them a new kind of jingle, so that your holiday is fulfilling and meaningful for you, and that your revived joy can send ripples throughout the world.

I don't ever want to downplay clinical depression or claim that this process can cure such a condition. I have learned that clinical depression can happen to anyone, at any time. I urge you, if you find yourself in a state of mind that doesn't seem to be helped by any positive thought, seek the help of a therapist. My process can be used in conjunction with the protocol recommended by your doctor or therapist.

CHAPTER 1

Scrooge

*"That is my name, and I fear it may
not be pleasant to you."*

The name in question is "Scrooge." At this point in the classic novel, *A Christmas Carol,* by Charles Dickens, a transformed Ebenezer Scrooge is apologetically approaching two men at whom he'd sneered, the previous day, as they collected charitable funds on Christmas Eve. Just prior to blasting them with his wintry chill, he'd chased a young Christmas caroler, mid "God Rest Ye Merry, Gentlemen," from his door. Indeed, the iconic name is synonymous with *heartless, mean, selfish miser.* The character of

Ebenezer Scrooge is so well known that if someone referred to you as a Scrooge, you would feel it more as a slap in the face than a pat on the back!

Charles Dickens shares this description of Scrooge:

Oh! But he was a tight-fisted hand at the grindstone, Scrooge! A squeezing, wrenching, grasping, scraping, clutching, covetous, old sinner! Hard and sharp as flint, from which no steel had ever struck out generous fire; secret, and self-contained, and solitary as an oyster. The cold within him froze his old features, nipped his pointed nose, shrivelled his cheek, stiffened his gait; made his eyes red, his thin lips blue; and spoke out shrewdly in his grating voice. A frosty rime was on his head, and on his eyebrows, and his wiry chin. He carried his own low temperature always about with him; he iced his office in the dog-days; and didn't thaw it one degree at Christmas.

And, yet, we love Scrooge, don't we? He's human. He's redeemable. I'll bet even the most cheerful among us can relate to his grumpiness and pain, if we're honest. When the Ghost of Christmas Past takes him back to his childhood, we are introduced to young Ebenezer in the midst of a sad, lonely childhood. Heaped on top of his mother's death, he feels the sting of being unloved and rejected by his father and excluded and abandoned by the other children in his boarding school. He feels happy for a brief time, while he is in love, but his deep-rooted fear and need for security lead to his extreme focus on making money. This obsession with money drives away one of the only bright lights in his life: the woman he loves. The other bright light was his sister Fan, who died young, but not before giving birth to Scrooge's nephew Fred.

Scrooge is a tragic, complicated figure. Although we may despise his lack of compassion for those less fortunate and his stinginess with his wealth, we might also understand his need to protect his heart. He was in so much pain that he installed as many locks upon that heart as he did his bedroom door.

I could've named this book *Helping Scrooge, Loving the Scrooge, Embracing Our Inner Scrooge,* or *Healing Scrooge*, but I chose not to. *Defeating Scrooge* speaks of the initial qualities we think of when we think of Scrooge: the dark, cold emptiness Ebenezer felt for most of his life, which prevented him from experiencing the joy of Christmas. It is not unlike the emptiness that we ourselves may be experiencing or want to protect our spirits against. *Defeating Scrooge* is about *taking intentional action to eclipse whatever threatens to rob us of our joy with brighter, newly inspired light.*

A popular dramatic theme is the rags-to-riches Cinderella story. Why? Because we delight in believing that we, too, can have such a makeover. In Scrooge's case, it's an emotional makeover. Begrudgingly, he steps out of his safety zone and opens his mind to a more meaningful experience. His jaw unclenches, his white-knuckled fists open, and his ice-cold, locked-up heart bursts open with gratitude, empathy, and, yes, even joy! Consciously or not, we recognize Scrooge's vulnerabilities, and we inhale the hope of such transformation for ourselves. But Scrooge was *pushed* to crack his protective shell and let in the light. He *had* to choose to open his mind or die. For us, it's not usually so black and white. But if we don't want our spirits to die, we too must open our minds, crack open our shells, and let the light of new discoveries add more meaning to our holiday experiences.

Deep down, we don't really want to defeat Scrooge, the human being. That would be like defeating ourselves! Don't we all have a degree of Scrooge in us? Haven't we also experienced feelings of fear, insecurity, rejection, loss, and abandonment? Haven't we seethed as we've pushed past jovial pedestrians, grumbled or hissed at people we felt were impeding us in some way, or secluded ourselves behind our locked gazes, arms, doors, or wallets because it felt safer than looking at our reflections in the eyes of others? Scrooge is both the antagonist and the protagonist in his story. I believe the same could be said for most of

Don't we all have a degree of Scrooge in us?

us. Once we consciously relate to Ebenezer, we want to help him. We want to put our arms around him and give him a big, long squeeze, against his protests and flailing, until he gives in and accepts that he is, indeed, lovable, loved, unique, and important on this earth.

Not surprisingly, Dickens invented the name Scrooge with a clever wink to an old English verb: To "scrouge" means "to squeeze." Yes, he squeezed his money and his heart. What are we squeezing?

Might I suggest that we give our inner Scrooge a big, warm, healing squeeze, until we—like Scrooge— come back around to the sentiment of Scrooge's nephew, Fred, who says:

> But I am sure I have always thought of Christmas time, when it has come round–apart from the veneration due to its sacred name and origin, if anything belonging to it can be apart from that–as a good time; a kind, forgiving, charitable, pleasant time; the only time I know

of, in the long calendar of the year, when men and women seem by one consent to open their shut-up hearts freely, and to think of people below them as if they really were fellow-passengers to the grave, and not another race of creatures bound on other journeys.

Are you ready to discover more meaning? Let's do this.

CHAPTER 2

My Story

I grew up in the beautiful state of Michigan, where white Christmases were not only dreamt of, but expected. My mother is a hearty woman who grew up in Ludington and received her swimming instruction at the hands of the rugged, thick-blooded Coast Guard cadets in the bone-chilling waters of Lake Michigan. She made sure that I spent lots of time in the snow with my brother Paul, my sister Brenda, and eventually my stepbrothers Gary and Steve. I remember us putting two layers of socks on our feet, followed by bread bags held up by rubber bands, and then our snow boots. We lived directly across the street from a small sand dune that we called "the hill." When it snowed, sledding was easily accessible and gave us hours of neighborhood fun, but I was not a big fan of playing out in the snow. I didn't realize that I had a condition called "cold urticaria" that caused me to want to scratch my skin off after spending time out in the cold. I thought everyone got itchy in the snow. I loved warming up afterward to hot cocoa and a crackling fire in the fireplace. To me, there was no sight more beautiful than a snowscape viewed from the warmer side of a window pane!

I was a day-dreaming, highly empathetic artist of a child with the soul of a poet and a desire to please. But the lens through which a child might see her circumstances is often convex. It magnifies and burns onto the retina of memory moments that make her feel like she is incapable of pleasing others. People who didn't know me as a child are surprised to learn that I had very little self-confidence back then. But when Advent would come around, something lifted me. Feelings of awe-inspiring, mysterious love enveloped me. I'd wake up in the middle of the night, when the rest of my family was asleep, and I'd tiptoe down the hall to the living room. I'd plug in the Christmas tree lights and sit on the floor by the tree, silently looking up at the sublime sight: the glorious, magnificent beauty of the colored lights twinkling and peeking out from the vibrant evergreen boughs, illuminating shiny glass ornaments and quivering strings of silver tinsel. The tree topper, reminiscent of the Star of Bethlehem, pointed upward to heaven. I'd look out the window where the lights were reflected, overlaying the blue, wintry scene of the moonlight dimly shining on the snow, as if hushed and careful not to waken it.

While sitting there, I would think about God, and how He created such beauty. I thought about how He also created me, and I felt His presence. I felt His support. Yes, I thought about the sweet little infant Jesus, but I thought more about the reactions and feelings of the people around this miracle—this incomprehensible gift of love sent to us. I'd think about Mary and Joseph, and their uncomfortable trip to Bethlehem. That reminded me of the times my family would look for a welcoming motel after traveling too late into the evening on summer vacations. I imagined their exhaustion and fear to think of more traveling before finding a vacancy.

I thought of the shock and vulnerability the shepherds must have felt when the angels appeared above them! What an honor it was for them to be the first to learn of the Savior's birth. How humble and amazed they must have been. And I thought about that dear old Saint, who knew about me and cared about me and who was so filled with Christmas joy that he wanted to celebrate with me by climbing down my chimney and giving me presents.

I'd sit there and feel the quiet awe of what that all meant, and about how much God loved me, no matter what was going on in my life. I was filled with joy that God sent to earth a gift of Love for all of us.

I have many happy memories of Christmastime with my family. We'd spend time together making push-pin and sequined ornaments and decorating cookies. I remember falling in love with "O Little Town of Bethlehem," which I was learning for our school's Christmas concert, and singing it in the car on the way to a holiday water fountain light show in Grand Haven. I'm sure I learned "Silent Night," "O Come All Ye Faithful," and "Angels We Have Heard On High" standing with my family in church. Through the car radio, the crooning of Bing Crosby and the deep, rich, sincere tones of Nat King Cole put me in reveries in the back seat as we motored to the mall for holiday shopping. Sitting in the living room with my siblings and watching the annual televised Christmas specials like "Merry Christmas, Charlie Brown," the Rankin-Bass musical Claymations, and The Walton's pilot movie, "The Homecoming," was a particular thrill for me. Carols were finding a home in the corridors of my heart.

My father was an air traffic controller who guided

planes to safe takeoffs and landings from the top of what is now called the Gerald Ford International Airport. One year, he had to work on Christmas morning. He tried to wake us kids up by blasting Christmas music from the living room stereo console. He had a lot of Christmas spirit! When I was 9, he died quite suddenly and unexpectedly of a brain aneurysm. That year, we had a different kind of Christmas—a sad Christmas. But there was still love, because Christmas was and is a time when we make more of an effort to show love, no matter what has happened throughout the year. Christmas felt like love to me. It still does.

No matter what has happened throughout the year. Christmas felt like love to me. It still does.

———————

* * *

I like to tell the story about how I became a vocal harmony singer. Vocal harmony is when people sing together, taking different notes in musical chords and singing them at the same time. Some people have trouble singing notes other than the melody line. Some people tend to gravitate to whatever musical notes a person near them is singing. It takes a bit of a practiced musical ear to stay strong and sing a different musical line than the people near you are singing, but I believe it's a craft worth cultivating. Some people have an especially keen ear for even difficult note intervals in musical chords. Here's how I think I became one of those people. Every weekend, my family attended church together. I'd stand right next to my mom, and when it came time to sing the hymns, let me tell you, she sang out to the Lord! As if a drill sergeant was standing over her, shouting "Louder! Higher!" People often ask me where I get my voice. Well, I have my mother's voice. But, thankfully, I don't have her ear.

If there was a high note coming, she'd just wing it up there somewhere, and it would usually land right on that note that would make the hair stand up on the back of your neck. We still laugh when we think about how people three pews up would turn around to see what that awful noise was. But I thought it was beautiful that, in spite of the fact that she had no reason to believe that singing was one of her gifts, she was putting such unabashed gusto into it for God. So, there I'd be, standing right next to her English-ambulance siren tones, trying very hard to decipher what chords the organ was playing on the other side of the church and singing within that chord. That turned out to be excellent ear training for me.

In this way, I sang my way through my childhood. I would spend solitary hours singing on my backyard swing. And I began to get a very strong feeling that I wanted to express myself through music in bigger ways. I even put together a small a cappella group in middle school. In high school, I took part in choirs, plays, musicals, and voice competitions, and I dreamed of moving to New York City and making a career out of using my voice there. I studied Musical Theatre at the University of Michigan.

When I finally arrived in The Big Apple, the city of my dreams, I was dismayed to see so much of what I called "frown pollution" everywhere. Here we were, in the greatest city in the world, and it seemed almost everybody was going around frowning. I

Here we were, in the greatest city in the world, and it seemed almost everybody was going around frowning.

began to dream of combatting the problem by creating a company that would bring joy to the city not only through our singing, but with random acts of kindness, or S.M.I.L.E.s; acts like bringing hot cocoa to cold construction workers in the dead of winter, singing at the firehouses for everyday heroes, caroler flash mobs, handing out hand warmers and Dunkin Donut gift cards to homeless people, and just taking more time giving disoriented tourists directions.

One November, I was asked to put together a small

group to carol at an event. I don't even remember saying "yes," but I do remember marching myself right down to City Hall. I started my company that day and named it "I SMILE in New York Productions." SMILE is an acronym for Shine My Inner Light Everywhere, and that's what we strive to do. We are never more successful at it than when we're out caroling.

The company took off quickly. We went from being a quartet our first year, to 12 of us, then 25. Now I have about 30 Broadway-trained carolers every year, and as many Victorian and other costumes as well. We typically perform in trios and quartets in groups called The Fabulous Fezziwigs, The Broadway CAREolers, and our Currier & Ives quartet. We carol at a variety of places from private parties to corporate events and landmark restaurants like The Lamb's Club to annual holiday events like the New York Botanical Gardens Holiday Train Show, and the Miracle on Madison Avenue, where the participating merchants donate a generous portion of their proceeds from the day to a charity.

SMILE is an acronym for Shine My Inner Light Everywhere, and that's what we strive to do. We are never more successful at it than when we're out caroling.

We delight in seeing faces light up when people see and hear us, and we invite them to sing with us. We love taking their requests for that special carol that will ignite their Christmas spirit. We truly feel that we are a part of what's special about New York City and the surrounding area during the holidays. We have had countless people tell us that their Christmas spirit kicked in for the first time that holiday season when they experienced caroling with us. Hearing that feeds our spirits, too.

People who know me know that I usually have Christmas spirit to spare. It was always there for me. But one year, something happened: my kids and I put up our Christmas tree, decorated it, and I noticed that I wasn't feeling my usual holiday spirit. I thought, *That's odd and disappointing, but it'll kick in.* I put a holiday movie on TV and poured us some eggnog. Still nothing. I unwrapped a candy cane and tasted it. No spark. Weird.

People who know me know that I usually have Christmas spirit to spare.

A couple of days later, my carolers and I had our first event of the season: an annual tree lighting at which we carol every year. It's a beautiful event where happy adults and wide-eyed children clad in velvet dresses or plaid vests gather around the carolers to see us in our beautiful costumes and hear us singing the ancient carols. At some point, the children are invited to flip a giant switch, illuminating the magnificent tree, and right on cue, we carolers burst into the joyous first verse of "O Christmas Tree."

Later, we visit each table in the great room where the glasses tink and the silverware clinks, and the conversation is buoyant and effervescent as groups of family and friends have an Advent luncheon. We ask each assembly if there is a favorite carol they would like to hear. It's always interesting to me to see how frequently the majority of guests at a table will turn to one person in particular to see what he or she would like to hear. I don't know what makes them do that, but I like to imagine.

Perhaps it's the family member who is roundly agreed upon to have the most Christmas spirit and who will surely request the perfect carol in a jolly way that will be remembered for years to come. Perhaps it's a person the family of whom is trying to tenderly cloak in love during a time of health or emotional challenge. Maybe it's the patriarch of the family who will feel disgruntled if he is not deferred to, and to keep the celebration cheerful, they obediently give him his druthers. Sometimes it's someone's birthday and filling their carol request is like a gift. Oftentimes, the whole table will turn to the youngest among them with animated faces, participating in the act of passing on the joy of holiday music to the next generation and eagerly anticipating the delight on their cherub faces.

My heart strings pull when I think about how family members may cherish memories of an aging matriarch's spirit from Christmases past, and are poignantly mindful that each holiday experience with her should be treasured. And so they look to her to see—what? A spark of delight that has been missing for a while? A flash of a memory that causes a quick intake of her breath? A recognition of the very special moment she and her family are experiencing presently? Each table has a story into which we carolers are privileged to get a glimpse.

Each table has a story into which we carolers are privileged to get a glimpse.

With determined, if not hopeful, recollections of this spirited event at the forefront of my mind, I loaded my Victorian costume, carol book, and basket of bells into my car (my car jingles all the way during the holidays). On the way there, I told myself, *This is the day my spirit will kick in. All I need is to carol with my friends, and get the guests singing with us, and the kids jingling the bells, and I'll be flooded with joy.*

And so, that morning, I found myself standing on the grand staircase with my fellow carolers, smiling and singing, and acting joyful, but a cold, growing fear was gnawing at me from inside. I still wasn't feeling that spirit. At one point, one of my carolers winked at me and suggested singing what he knew was my favorite carol, "Good King Wenceslas." I appreciated the gesture and the story the carol tells. But it didn't unlock my elusive spirit. I heard a voice inside me say, *It should have.*

As the season rolled along, the silence of my Christmas spirit was deafening. Like the hot pulsing

As the season rolled along, the silence of my Christmas spirit was deafening.

of blood to a fingertip struck by a hammer, it seemed my spirit had suffered such an injury, and it stung. It ached with a pounding that would not be ignored. It felt like the senseless passing of a loved one. But there was no time for mourning and examining until that year's holidays were in the rearview mirror. Until then, I had to rely on my theatrical training to reach outside of my pain, don a gay appearance, and provide a joyful experience for those around me. Never had I imagined myself singing "Joy to the World" but feeling like Scrooge on the inside. But there I was. Ouch.

* * *

January came around. Hardly aware of the dry pine needles pricking my fingers before falling to the floor as I unhooked each ornament and put it back in the box, I asked myself, *What happened? Where did my Christmas spirit go? What was different about this year than all of my previous years?*

I continued to puzzle through my dilemma as I unplugged each string of lights, pulled the beaded garlands from the boughs, and made multiple trips up and down the step stool to lower the star and unwind the cold, electrical strands. I traced my way backward through the previous year, leading up to this just-past melancholic holiday season. My life had seemed normal enough. My attempts to improve my marriage were no more or less successful than in previous years, as far as I knew. My children were both in good health and full of enthusiasm for their chosen activities. My caroling company was thriving. What, then? I continued to backtrack. I had gotten all the way back to the previous January when it struck me between the eyes. A shock and betrayal I had experienced a full 11 months

A shock and betrayal I had experienced a full 11 months prior to December had taken its toll and wounded my soul, which damaged my spirit.

prior to December had taken its toll and wounded my soul, which damaged my spirit.

A couple of years earlier, I'd befriended someone. I'd been warned by a few people that she was not to be trusted, but I believed everyone deserves forgiveness and second chances. Just look at the company Jesus kept! I was a good friend to her. I forgave her for what I thought were little transgressions throughout those two years. I may have been the best friend she had. That January, I learned that my family and I had been violated in a criminal way. I was stunned and heartbroken to learn that she was the one trying to hurt us. Dozens of people came forward to tell me the hurtful and untrue things she had been saying about me and my family for the two years we had known each other. These accounts echoed the things that were said on the two separate social media pages that impersonated one of my minor children. "Do unto others as you would have them do unto you," and, "Forgive seventy times seven times," echoed in my mind. Hadn't I forgiven her over and over? Hadn't I treated her the way I would have wanted to be treated? Yes. Yes, I had. So how could this happen to my family? One of the rocks of my faith had been cracked. And into that crack seeped some tainted toxin that corrupted my Christmas spirit like malware on my laptop.

I hadn't realized until this time just how important my Christmas spirit had been to me. I now realized that I had unconsciously relied on the holidays to recharge my spiritual battery for the coming year. My Christmas spirit had been helping me start each year with faith in my fellow humans and hope for light and love in the new year. This particular January, a full year after my

I now realized that I had unconsciously relied on the holidays to recharge my spiritual battery for the coming year.

traumatic experience, I was feeling dark, cold, empty, and sad. There was nothing in my spiritual reserve.

I simply could not let this stand. This was unacceptable! I knew I had to take immediate, intentional action to revive my spirit, and tend to it all through the year so that it would be there for me when I most needed it. But what?

As I bent forward to sweep the dead pine needles into the dust pan, I found my nose inches from a box that housed a caroler's top hat with a carol book lying on top of it. *I wonder . . .*, I thought.

I picked up the book and started flipping through the pages of carols I'd been singing for years. Could the answer be in there?

My heart quickened. Right then and there, I set

a goal for myself: I would concentrate on a different carol each week of the year and examine the carols in ways I never had before. Yes, I knew a lot about the carols, but it suddenly occurred to me that there was much more to discover, and maybe, just maybe, I would revive my dormant spirit by discovering some of those things. I knew within the very first week that it was working. The magic of the holiday spirit was rekindling. I learned about the composers, lyricists, the times and places in which the carols were written, and the motivations, joys, and heartaches from which they were born. I found that the carols have taken on a life of their own long after their creators have left this earth. The history of each of these carols is still being written today! And I'm part of that history. If you're reading this book, you are too!

What did I do about my friend, you may ask? I timidly confronted her. She denied the undeniable, and then I did my best to forgive her one more time and then move on and away from her. But you see, the exact nature of my spirit-damaging event isn't important. It only matters that it happened, and spirit-damaging events can happen to anyone at any time. Every holiday season there are people trying to summon joy or some semblance of peace while they are grieving the loss of a loved one, enduring treatment in the face of a grave diagnosis, facing the fear and uncertainty of a career setback, reeling over teenagers who have gone off the rails, confronting the sting of feeling excluded from holiday traditions, and so many more reasons. Many people suffer during the holidays.

I invite you to join me on this journey through the carols. I've included some of my discoveries, thoughts, and applications in this book. I hope my journey captures your imagination and ignites new sparks to fuel your holiday spirit.

CHAPTER 3

God Rest You Merry, Gentlemen

Beginning the journey

The day I set out on my journey through the carols, I picked up my carol book and sat down in a comfortable, but not too comfortable chair. I had decided to let prayer and meditation inspire which carols I would choose when, so I set about clearing my mind to meditate. I was not in the habit of meditating. I was afraid I might fall asleep. I had heard about how to meditate for many years, so I set my kitchen timer for 10 minutes, and I concentrated on my breath coming into my lungs. I was as mindful as possible of my breath as I slowly exhaled. My mind began to wander, but I remembered to gently push each stowaway thought aside and get back to focusing on my breathing. Ten minutes went by in a flash but also gave me the feeling that I'd stolen time or multiplied minutes in my day. On top of that, I felt focused and alert.

I have always felt a comforting presence with me, which I know in my heart to be God. I go through every day talking to this constant help and companion. On this day, after my meditation, I spent a few minutes thanking God for specific blessings in my life and, in particular, for this idea which I felt was heaven-sent. I asked God to bless this endeavor and show me what I needed to see when I needed to see it. Then I asked God to show me the first carol I was to work on. I opened my book randomly, and there was "God Rest You Merry Gentlemen."

I asked God to bless this endeavor and show me what I needed to see when I needed to see it.

I've always liked this carol, its minor key and energetic pace. I looked at the lyrics:

God Rest You Merry, Gentlemen
Let nothing you dismay:
Remember Christ our savior
Was born on Christmas Day,
To save us all from Satan's pow'r
When we had gone astray;

O tidings of comfort and joy, comfort and joy,
O tidings of comfort and joy.

From God our heav'nly Father
A blessed angel came,
And unto certain shepherds
Brought tidings of the same;
How that in Bethlehem was born
The Son of God by name;

O tidings of comfort and joy, comfort and joy,
O tiding of comfort and joy.

Now to the Lord sing praises,

All you within this place,
And with true love and brotherhood
Each other now embrace;
This holy tide of Christmas all others doth efface,

O tidings of comfort and joy, comfort and joy,
O tiding of comfort and joy.

Composer and lyricist unknown
Year written thought to be 16th century or earlier
Earliest known printing of the carol was on a broadsheet in 1760
First known publishing by E. F. Rimbault, 1846
First known text publishing in collection in
Christmas Carols Ancient and Modern, William Sandys, 1833
The carol is referred to in *A Christmas Carol*, by Charles Dickens, 1843

On this first day of my journey, I opted to simply decide on the carol of the week, look at the lyrics and think about them, let them bounce around my head for the rest of the day and consider: What do I think the song is saying? Do I know what all of the words mean?

"God Rest You, Merry Gentlemen
Let nothing you dismay"

It took me by surprise that I couldn't even get past the first line with any certainty, yet, I'd been singing this carol my whole life! Is it a wish for God to give a group of merry gentlemen a nap? A good night's sleep? Or to put their fears to rest? Who are these merry gentlemen? Are they similar to Robin Hood's band of merry men? Are they merry like Santa Claus or Old King Cole? I decided that I thought it was a wish to a group of men (or people) that they should put their fears to rest and be glad while remembering that Christ the Savior was born. I did take note that this interpretation would mean that the traditional comma after the "you" would actually be in the wrong place. But I didn't care. I decided I would look up the history of the carol and the etymology of the words "rest" and "merry" the next day.

I felt a welcome tinge of glee. Already I was making Christmas discoveries, even if those discoveries were simply that I had discoveries to make!

The next day, I surfed the internet and looked up the carol. I found a story quoted in an article that made me dizzy with delight. The excerpt was from a book of interesting backstories of carols. Perfect! Exactly what I needed to help me on my journey. This story addressed the etymology of the words and even the comma in the title.

Already I was making Christmas discoveries, even if those discoveries were simply that I had discoveries to make!

_____

I was so fascinated by this story, it felt like I was reading a thriller.

It told me that, back in the early 15th century, many churchgoers really didn't like the music that was presented in churches at the time, and laypeople had no say in the matter. So, they started writing songs that reflected their faith that they would then sing and play in their homes. These early Christmas folk songs are the foundation of what we now consider Christmas carols. Imagine, the peasant class during the 1400s, dutifully going to church, but then going home and leading a sort of quiet rebellion against the dreary tone of the current church music and celebrating the stories of the Bible *their* way.

"God Rest Ye Merry, Gentlemen" wasn't allowed in churches for hundreds of years. It wasn't published until the 1800s and that was due to Queen Victoria's love of these songs that reflected a more layman-friendly worship of God and celebration of Christmas. I imagined that is one of the reasons the Victorian era is ever-present in even our current traditions, including my storage unit full of costumes for my Victorian caroling groups called The Fabulous Fezziwigs.

I was eager to find out what the carol meant. My eyes must have grown wide when I read that there is a misunderstood word we've been associating with Christmas for the longest time: merry. I have always thought of it as a charming, old fashioned way of saying "happy." It's just more fun to say, "Merry Christmas" than "Happy Christmas," right? I have to admit, I love to think of Santa Claus and his rosy cheeks and twinkling, merry eyes. As dear as those sentimental feelings I had attached to the word were, I now had another layer to add that made a huge difference.

Back in medieval times, the word "merry" actually meant "mighty." It made the nursery rhyme of Old King Cole, that "merry old soul," seem less ridiculous. And although I got a kick out of the giddy cinematic *SHREK* parody of Robin Hood's merry men, it now seemed he actually had a band of *mighty* men.

Another word that needed interpreting was "rest." Back then, it meant "make" or "keep." Also, it seemed to be agreed upon that the comma has been misplaced all of these years. So according to this book, what this title really meant was, "God Make you Mighty, Gentlemen," or, "God Keep You Mighty, Gentlemen. Let nothing you dismay. Remember Christ our Savior was born on Christmas Day!"

I loved that idea. I still do. You could sing that at any time of year, the idea being, "I know things are hard right now, but stay strong. Remember Christ was born to save us!"

I started thinking about how we could start wishing each other not just a happy Christmas, but a *Mighty Christmas.* How would we celebrate differently if we were trying to have a Mighty Christmas?"

My spirit was soaring to learn of these gems that lay behind this carol! I ordered the book about carols, and another one from this author. I was ravenous to learn more. I could already feel my spirit being revived, and I eagerly jumped into my second week's carol . . .

How would we celebrate differently if we were trying to have a Mighty Christmas?

Looking back on that first day of my journey through the carols, I'm glad that I started by praying that simple prayer for God to show me what I needed to see when I needed to see it. What I read about the Olde English meaning of the word "merry" was just what I needed to jump-start the rebirth of my joy, and propel me, purposefully, forward into this process, which has saved and nurtured my spirit continually ever since.

If I had read back then that this definition of the word was disputed, and in fact seems to be disproven altogether, I might have felt too discouraged to continue. By the time I learned that there is no evidence to support merry meaning mighty, I was already energized about the idea of Christmas being mighty.

My subsequent study of other carols further convinced me that Christmas is, indeed, mighty. Christmas is strong, and I believe its spirit has the power to bring about more peace in our world. Read on. You'll see what I mean.

And by the way, I still ask, "How would we celebrate differently, if we were trying to have a Mighty Christmas?"

CHAPTER 4

Good King Wenceslas

YE WHO NOW WILL BLESS THE POOR

Good King Wenceslas looked out on the Feast of Stephen
When the snow lay round about, deep and crisp and even.
Brightly shone the moon that night, tho the frost
    was cruel,
When a poor man came in sight gathering winter fuel.

"Hither page and stand by me. If thou know'st it telling
Yonder peasant, who is he? Where and what his dwelling?"
"Sire he lives a good league hence, underneath
    the mountain
Right against the forest fence, by St. Agnus fountain."

"Bring me flesh and bring me wine. Bring me pine
    logs hither!

Thou and I will see him dine, when we bear them thither."
Page and monarch forth they went. Forth they
    went together.
Through the rude wind's wild lament and the
    bitter weather.

"Sire the night is darker now, and the wind
    blows stronger.
Fails my heart, I know not how. I can go no longer."
"Mark my footsteps, my good page! Tread thou in
    them boldly.
Thou shalt find the winter's rage freeze thy blood
    less coldly."

In his master's steps he trod where the snow lay dinted.
Heat was in the very sod which the saint had printed.
Therefore Christian men be sure, wealth or
    rank possessing,
Ye who now will bless the poor shall yourselves
    find blessing.

First published in 1853
Words by John M. Neale (1818–1866)
Tune: Tempus Adest Floridum, a spring hymn from the
collection Piae Cantiones Published in 1582

When I began doing some research into the origins of this carol, I was glad to learn that Good King Wenceslas (also known as *Wenceslas I*, *Wenceslaus I*, and *Vaclav the Good*) was based on some historical facts. He was actually a benevolent Duke of Bohemia, and because he went out every day, touching the lives of the poorest among them, he was so beloved that he was given the title of king posthumously.

Wenceslas was born a twin. In the many historical accounts I've read, I've seen his birth date recorded as 903 and 907 and his death as 929 or 935. Not surprisingly, there are more discrepancies, including the idea that his name may have actually been Vaclav. Although some critics of John Mason Neale's lyrics question why this is considered a Christmas carol, I find that relating it to Christmas spirit is natural. Putting aside the fact that the Feast of St. Stephen falls on the second day of Christmas, all I need to remember to consider this carol worthy of Christmas is that Wenceslas lived by the hallmarks of what many consider Christmas spirit: charity, mercy, being aware of the needs and feelings of others, being of service to others, and sharing joy.

He was born just a few minutes before his brother, Boleslas (some called him, "Boleslas the Cruel" or "Boleslas the Bad"). They were the sons of Duke Vratislaus. The Duke's mother (the twins' grandmother), Ludmilla, was a woman of deep Christian faith, and she was the primary caregiver of Wenceslas. It was she who instilled in him the importance of faith, hope, and charity. The twins' pagan mother, Drahomira, was the primary caregiver of Boleslas. In the year 921, their father was killed in battle, and Wenceslas became the ruler of Bohemia, with his Christian beliefs guiding him.

In what conjures up a dramatic biblical story, Wenceslas' mother and brother led a pagan revolt against him and assassinated Grandmother Ludmilla as she prayed! He was just a teenager, but Wenceslas was able to overcome the rebellion and astounded his subjects by mercifully exiling Drahomira and Boleslas rather than executing them.

In spite of his youth, Wenceslas was credited with the wisdom of Solomon as he set up a nation built on true justice and mercy. His goal was to serve his Lord through the laws he enacted. As the verses suggest, he really did go out into the country, meet with his subjects, and inquire about their needs. He had a heart for the poor, and not only urged his wealthier subjects to reach out to them, but he shared what he had with them.

It is said he truly loved Christmas. Centuries before it was a tradition to give Christmas gifts, he had a yearly ritual of going out into the country the day after Christmas (as some European countries called it "the second day of Christmas," Boxing Day, and the Feast of St. Stephen), bringing gifts of food, clothes, and firewood to the poorest of his subjects. Even when the weather was "frightful," and his men tried to persuade him to postpone his trip, he couldn't be stopped, just as the carol says. His inspiring example won many pagans over to Christianity.

He may have even been responsible for the conversion of his pagan brother. Boleslas had assembled some thugs and had them assassinate Wenceslas as he was going into church one day (some accounts say he was going into a party). Boleslas quickly regretted what he'd set in motion. In fact, it is said that he was devastated. Legend has it that Boleslas had a son born at the very moment Wenceslas was murdered, and Boleslas repented and dedicated the life of his son to Christianity and saw to it that he received a clergyman's education. He also had a daughter who became a nun. As the new ruler, Boleslas insisted on keeping the Christian ways Wenceslas had put in place and made it his mission to perpetuate his brother's legacy. It is because of the brother who had him murdered that we know of Wenceslas and his charitable ways today.

Wenceslas was canonized and honored with the title of king posthumously, by the Holy Roman Emperor Otto I. As the beloved patron saint of the Czech state, he is remembered as a charitable, merciful, Christmas-loving king who led countless people to Christ.

REFLECTIONS

When we're out caroling and we turn the page in our book to "Good King Wenceslas," invariably, my cohorts will announce that this is my favorite carol. And it is! I have always been touched by the heart of this kindly soul, this character who seemed to be a precursor to St. Nicholas.

I know a wonderful woman. Let's call her Hannah. Kind, thoughtful, and mindful. I was talking to her about my exploration of Christmas spirit and she let out a sound somewhere between a wail and a moan, with something between a gasp and a sigh in there as well. I got the feeling that the thought of Christmas was not a pleasant thought for Hannah.

I got the feeling that the thought of Christmas was not a pleasant thought for Hannah.

Her dismay surprised me. I have known Hannah since she was a child, and I receive an annual Christmas family photo of her and her family that I tape up with the holiday greeting cards my family receives. It is always a joyful photo—gobs of family gathered together in their coordinated, festive clothing, smiling, hugging, holding hands in some glorious, nature-oriented scene. My immediate thought is always, *Wow! Look how much they love to spend time together. They must really be doing something right to not only want to travel the miles and go to the expense to be together at Christmastime, but to also have the spirit to cooperate with each other, finding the matching clothes, and whatever Christmas costuming doodads had been decided upon that year!* I have to admit, I was envious. I, myself, was lucky if I could get a photo of my kids by the tree on Christmas morning, in PJs, messy hair, and puffy eyes that were actually open!

I asked her if she wouldn't mind telling me where that guttural sound came from. She was eager to explain. What she told me helped me in ways she couldn't have foreseen.

Hannah has an amazing mother. Hannah is the first to heap praise upon her. I also happen to adore this super mom. She is one of these creatures whose heart is too big for her rib cage. She is always thinking about the needs and feelings of others and puts those people before herself. Therefore, it probably won't surprise you to learn that Hannah's mom—let's call her Grace—started an organization to help less fortunate people have a more joyful Christmas. Or at least a less barebones Christmas, and more of the kind of Christmas that is expected in today's Western world. You know, the kind of holiday reflected in catalogs, TV commercials, and (now) Facebook. Let's call that organization "Grace's Basement."

Now, everyone can agree that being of service to others and sharing this tradition with one's children is a good thing, right? And Grace did get her children involved. They would gather gift donations for the less fortunate and store them in Grace's basement. There they would wrap them, put festive ribbons and gift tags on them, and lovingly send them out on Christmas Eve. What a lovely effort, right? What could be better for the world and for the enrichment of our children? Every year, Grace's Basement grew bigger. More families in need were added to their list. More people from churches, communities, neighborhoods, and other organizations donated gifts. Grace's basement was practically bursting at the seams with toys, gadgets, clothes, tubes of wrapping paper, spools of ribbon, tags, and tape.

As Hannah got older, she became more and more involved in this mission. When she was in high school, she did about as much as her mom did, and, increasingly, it was adding stress to the beautiful holiday they knew as Christmas. December had now become a month of frantic deadlines, messy house, holiday clutter everywhere, undone laundry, dishes in the sink, no counter space, constant phone ringing, tense smiles, and tight chests. There was no time to go to the Botanical Garden and take in the holiday lights together or to see a holiday show or even go out and have a walk through the park as a family. Hannah got to the point where she wished her family could escape Grace's Basement—just for one year—and (figuratively speaking) go up to the living room and have a quiet Christmas season by themselves.

And then Hannah went to college. One day, she received a call from her mom about what the family would be wearing for the holiday photo, and the date during the Thanksgiving holiday when that would be taken. Hannah dutifully put her ensemble together. She found a red sweater, a white skirt, and boot-lets. Grace always supplied the Santa hats. Hannah, sadly, declined requests for visits with old school friends for that weekend, but the family did gather together, had a lovely Thanksgiving meal, and went out to a clearing in the woods to take the photo. And it was beautiful. Grace took charge of sending the photos to family and friends in time for the Christmas delivery.

With her kids in college, Grace had taken on more and more hours at her job, and when Hannah came home for winter break, Grace had a to-do list for her. One year, much to Hannah's surprise—and dismay—she found that she, herself, was now the chief coordinator, present-wrapper, gift tag signer, and deliverer for Grace's Basement. A huge job that Grace was too busy to handle even a little bit of that year. Hannah jumped in and did the job, but she felt pings of resentment. What's worse, after her graduation from college, she learned that her mother was still expecting her to travel back home, every year,

Hannah felt trapped, bitter, and totally out of touch with the spirit that used to fill her with joy and wonder during her childhood Christmases

———

and help with the charity in the same ways. Hannah felt trapped, bitter, and totally out of touch with the spirit that used to fill her with joy and wonder during her childhood Christmases.

Hannah pretended to have mixed feelings when Grace's basement was taken over by other people, but secretly, it was a relief for her. Hannah was now married, and she and her husband had children of their own. They no longer lived close to her mother, but she still felt the matriarchal pressure from her, every year, to pack up her family, buy the requisite photo apparel for her family, and travel the miles to celebrate Christmas together. This pressure was made more intense by the fact that Grace insisted on paying the airfare for the entire family. It felt like more of an obligation than a celebration. Her husband once called it a "sentence"; Hannah found herself nodding. For Hannah, the spirit of Christmas had become one of anxiety and resentment.

These days, Hannah wishes for a Christmas tucked away with her husband and kids in a little cabin in the woods somewhere, with no one telling them what to wear, how to celebrate or with whom, or what their obligations are.

I have to confess that I relate to Grace a little too much in this story. And I wonder how much I have imposed my own desire to share that spirit of Christmas charity with others, possibly even to the point of sapping the joy right out of the season for my own family.

As I run a caroling company, hints of Christmas start taking over the house early in the year. The auditions take place at the end of the summer. Pages and stacks of music cover the dining room table and kitchen counter tops for weeks. Phone calls, emails, and texts increase dramatically as rehearsals begin in the autumn, and people contact me to book the carolers for holiday tree lightings, shopping district promotions, festivals of lights, and holiday celebrations. Up to 30 costumes are laid out all over certain rooms as I check them for repair needs, assign them to carolers, and arrange to deliver them. And, then, just as the holiday music and decorations start popping up all over town, I'm either running off to add joy to celebrations for other people's families to enjoy, or receiving calls and texts from carolers and clients, and managing the coordination of those events, remotely, possibly interrupting the seasonal joy my family might be experiencing together.

We do have Christmas traditions that we take time to observe. Christmas Eve and Christmas Day are two days that I—except in case of a caroling emergency—do not work as a caroler myself. It is all about being together as a family. I'm glad we have that. But I can't help but wonder what other quiet traditions I could have carved out time for. Now that my kids are young adults who are still with me during Christmas, I wonder if I can delegate some of the "busyness" of Christmas to others and help my family nurture a sense of Christmas *peace*—a figurative cabin in the woods, where we could gather winter fuel and imagine the saintly spirit whose charitable giving was not frenzied, but simply full of heart.

CHAPTER 5

O Holy Night

The Weary Soul Rejoices

Ok, let's go to France now! In 1847, there was an educated poet named Placide Cappeau, who was the commissionaire of wines in the small French town of Roquemaure. "Commissionaire" sounds rather fancy, but it seems to have been a uniformed position of service, like hotel concierge. At any rate, Cappeau was asked by his parish priest to write a poem for Christmas mass. Cappeau took on the assignment. Once he finished it, he decided that his "Cantique de Noel" was not just a poem, but a song, so he asked his musician friend Adolphe Charles Adams to compose music for the song.

That's one account of the story. Another is that Cappeau was about to take a business trip to Paris when his parish priest asked him to write the poem and take it with him to Paris to give to Adams, who was at the height of his success as a ballet and opera composer, and ask him to put it to music. In this version, Cappeau did not yet know Adams. Whichever story is correct, Adams agreed and composed the soaring music for the poem within a few days' time. Cappeau's church in Roquemaure debuted the glorious carol which is the most-requested of my carolers every single December.

The history of this carol is fascinating, involving the religious beliefs of both the lyricist and the composer, and how the carol almost faded into obscurity until it was discovered by an American who, during the Civil War, was moved by the abolitionist message in one of the verses and introduced it to a much wider audience. I will leave that for you, my reader, to discover on your own. (Or discover it in a future edition of *Defeating Scrooge*.) There is so much to discover and ponder in each one of the carols. For now, I'd like to

There is so much to discover and ponder in each one of the carols.

aim the viewfinder on an aspect of this story I think is seldom, if ever, considered.

Cappeau had only one hand—his left. He lost his right hand at the age of 8 when he and a friend found a gun and decided to play with it. His friend's father, the gun's owner, felt terrible about it and paid Cappeau's way through school, and, no doubt, it was Cappeau's education that helped him to become the poignant poet he grew to be.

If this terrible accident hadn't happened, and Cappeau hadn't come to know the depth of feeling that comes with such loss, and wasn't forced to find work and recreation for himself that didn't require the use of two hands, and the friend's father hadn't paid his way through school, he may not have become a world-class poet and we wouldn't have one of the most inspiring carols, still cherished all over the world, that we have in "O Holy Night." I do marvel when I think of how we shake our fists at the heavens and get angry at God for letting bad things happen to us. And then, maybe years later, we come to realize that God's plan for us was much bigger than we ever could have imagined.

Fast forward, now, to Christmas Eve 1870, in the midst of fierce fighting between the armies of Germany and France, during the Franco-Prussian War. A French soldier suddenly jumped out of his trench. Imagine what soldiers on each side must have thought! They could've thought, "He's crazy and a danger. Shoot him now!" But he stood there with no weapon in his hand or at his side. He lifted his eyes to the sky and started singing "Cantique de Noel."

Here, is the English translation of what he sang:

O Holy Night!
The stars are brightly shining
It is the night of the dear Savior's birth!
Long lay the world in sin and error pining
Till he appear'd and the soul felt its worth.
A thrill of hope the weary soul rejoices
For yonder breaks a new and glorious morn!

Fall on your knees
Oh hear the angel voices
Oh night divine
Oh night when Christ was born
Oh night divine
Oh night divine

Led by the light of Faith serenely beaming
With glowing hearts by His cradle we stand
So led by light of a star sweetly gleaming
Here come the wise men from Orient land
The King of Kings lay thus in lowly manger
In all our trials born to be our friend
He knows our need
To our weakness no stranger
Behold your king
Before him Lowly bend
Behold your king
Before him Lowly bend

Truly He taught us to love one another
His law is love and His gospel is peace
Chains shall He break for the slave is our brother
And in His name all oppression shall cease
Sweet hymns of joy in grateful chorus raise we,
Let all within us praise His holy name
Christ is the Lord
His power and glory ever more proclaim
His power and glory ever more proclaim

Written in French, 1847
Translated to English, 1855
Lyrics: Placide Cappeau (1808–1877)
Music: Adolphe Charles Adams (1803–1853)
English Translator: John Sullivan Dwight (1813–1893)

After completing all three verses, a German infantryman climbed out his of his trench and answered with Martin Luther's "From Heaven Above to Earth I Come."

Here is the English translation of his musical response:

From heav'n above to earth I come,
to bear good news to ev'ry home;
glad tidings of great joy I bring
whereof I now will say and sing:

To you, this night, is born a Child
of Mary, chosen mother mild;
this tender Child of lowly birth
shall be the joy of all the earth.

'Tis Christ our God, who far on high
had heard your sad and bitter cry;

Himself will your Salvation be,
Himself from sin will make you free.
Now let us all, with gladsome cheer,
follow the shepherds, and draw near
to see this wondrous Gift of God,
who hath His own dear Son bestowed.

Glory to God in highest heav'n,
who unto us His Son has giv'n,
while angels sing, with pious mirth,
a glad New Year to all the earth.

Year written: 1535
Text inspired by: Luke 2:1-18
Lyrics: Martin Luther (1483–1546)
Tune: Von Himmel hock, da Komm'ich her
Translated to English: Catherine Winkworth, 1855

The story goes that the fighting stopped for the next 24 hours while the men on both sides observed a temporary peace in honor of Christmas.

REFLECTIONS

How amazed might Cappeau have been to know that his words, penned with his remaining hand, would inspire enemy soldiers to throw their guns down? It's not likely he could have foreseen such divine irony the role weapons would play in his story.

When I look back on my life so far, I see so many events that seemed like unanswered prayers at the time, but for which I now thank God. These days, I sometimes find myself stubbornly demanding that my own will be done. Sometimes, I see bad things happening around me that scare me, that my most Herculean efforts cannot improve. I've lain awake in bed with my heart racing, unable to sleep for fear of the well-being of people I dearly love. I have only learned during the worst of these nights, when no amount of meditation slows my pounding heart, that handing my control of the situation over to and trusting in God is my truest and only failsafe path to peace.

It wasn't when I prayed, "God, please make this happen or let that happen" that I found peace. It was when I prayed, "God, you know my heart, and the hearts of my loved ones. I trust You. I trust that You love us and hold us in the palm of Your hand. I'm letting go of trying to control this situation, and I'm thanking You in advance for using this situation so that Your plan—which is greater than I can imagine—can unfold. Your will be done." It is in these worst of times, when I feel at my weakest, that I am able to see and feel the strong grace of God.

When I wake up the next morning after such a night and realize how quickly I fell asleep after surrendering to God, it is nothing short of a "new and glorious morn!" I also marvel at how the situations that worried me so would then resolve. I trust that God will put our struggles during times of trial to good use. Who knows? There might even be a chain reaction that causes our stories to shine a light for others, hundreds of years from now. What I do know is that when I remember that God loves us so very much, my weary soul rejoices.

CHAPTER 6

O Come,
All Ye Faithful

Building Bridges

In the year 1731, John Francis Wade, a Roman Catholic priest in England, found himself facing imprisonment or death, simply for practicing his faith in the years following "The Glorious Revolution." This event, also called The Revolution of 1688, was the deposition of the Roman Catholic King, James II, and the establishment of parliament as the majority ruling power of England in tandem with the monarch. It was called glorious because it was a bloodless overthrow. However, it was exclusionary in that it barred Roman Catholics from the throne. It also renewed the collective memories of persecution and executions of Catholics in the kingdom.

Being a devout man who put his faith first, Wade chose to become an exile of conscience rather than hide or denounce that faith. He fled to France. France was fairly bursting at the seams with Catholic priests in the same predicament at this tumultuous time, but Wade had an additional skill set that landed him in an important job at a critical time. This holy man of God was also a musician and skilled calligrapher. Many of the church records had been lost or destroyed during the conflict between the Roman Catholic Church and the Church of England. Wade found sanctuary in the Benedictine Abbey in Douai and was called upon to find and identify the old, cherished church music and meticulously catalogue and preserve it. It was during this time, perhaps inspired by this work, that he composed a sacred carol that is sung by masses of Christmas celebrators and is one of the most-requested of my caroling groups.

John Francis Wade wrote "Adeste Fideles" in Latin; it was translated to English as "O Come, All Ye Faithful." It is commonly sung in English with the

Latin first verse included at either the beginning or the end.

Adeste, fideles,
Laeti triumphantes,
Venite, venite in Bethlehem!
Natum videte,
Regem angelorum
Venite, adoremus!
Venite, adoremus!
Venite, adoramus Dominum!

O come, all ye faithful, joyful and triumphant,
O come ye, O come ye to Bethlehem!
Come, and behold Him, born the King of angels!

Refrain:
O come, let us adore Him;
O come, let us adore Him;
O come, let us adore Him, Christ, the Lord!

Sing, choirs of angels; sing in exultation;
sing, all ye citizens of heav'n above!
Glory to God, all glory in the highest! [Refrain]

Yea, Lord, we greet Thee, born this happy morning;
Jesus, to Thee be all glory giv'n!
Word of the Father, now in flesh appearing! [Refrain]

Year written: 1744
Words and music: John Francis Wade (1711–1786)

Fast forward to the Western Front of World War I, on Christmas Eve of 1914. A Christmas miracle occurred. This verified historical event is called "The

Christmas Truce of 1914." The setting: two trenches spanning 400 miles from the Swiss border of Germany and France to the North Sea. In one trench, the Germans, and British allied forces in the other. The distance between the warring trenches varied from as much as 100 feet to as little as 30 feet. Soldier's letters and interviews in articles from a variety of newspapers tell the amazing story.

Cpl. Leon Harris, from the 13th Battalion of the London Regiment, wrote,

"This has been the most wonderful Christmas I have ever struck. We were in the trenches on Christmas Eve, and about 8:30, the firing was almost at a standstill. Then the Germans started shouting across to us, 'a happy Christmas' and commenced putting up lots of Christmas trees with hundreds of candles on the parapets of their trenches."

Some recall that they first heard singing floating from the German trench. Some remember "Stille Nacht" ("Silent Night") first, others remember "O Holy Night," sung in German. The Brits knew that baring one's head above the trench could mean death, but peek over they did and saw what must've been a magical sight.

Pvt. G. Layton, of the A Company in the 1st Royal Warwickshire Regiment, wrote, "We would sing a song or a carol first and then they would sing one and I tell you they can harmonize all right."

The British forces would listen to the Germans sing a carol, in their native tongue, from down within their trench, and then the Brits would sing one in return, in English, from their trench. Back and forth the serenading went, and then, when the Germans starting singing "Adeste Fidelis" in the original Latin, the Brits joined together with them.

The Brits knew that baring one's head above the trench could mean death, but peek over they did and saw what must've been a magical sight.

———

Graham William of the Fifth London Rifle Brigade said, "And I thought, well, this is really a most extraordinary thing—two nations both singing the same carol in the middle of a war."

Between the many accounts of this most humanitarian moment in history, we learn about the soldiers trusting each other enough to climb out of their trenches and over the barbed wire, meeting each other in the middle of what was called "no man's land," shaking hands, exchanging gifts, and beginning to understand each other as fellow human beings. They pledged to each other not to shoot, but to spend Christmas as friends. They exchanged addresses and names and vowed to contact each other after the war. They gave each other time to bury their dead. They sang. They danced. They shared food and drink. They had bicycle races on bikes without tires, found in the ruins. Also found in the ruins were hats and umbrellas and other items they used as costumes to make each other laugh. Famously, they engaged each other in a friendly game of football, or soccer, as we Americans say.

One soldier wrote home, "Really you would hardly have thought we were at war. Here we were, enemy talking to enemy. They like ourselves with mothers, with wives waiting to welcome us home again. And to think within a few hours we shall be firing at each other again."

On the evening of December 26, after nearly 48 hours of recognizing and celebrating the common goodness between them, they did start firing at each other again. But it wasn't their choice or wish to do so.

"If we had been left to ourselves there would never have been another shot fired."

———

A soldier named Murdoch M. Wood gave a statement to the British parliament in 1930, "I then came to the conclusion that I have held very firmly ever since, that if we had been left to ourselves there would never have been another shot fired."

Some British superior officers, having gotten word of the fraternizing with the enemy, were outraged and not only threatened to court martial the soldiers, but fired the first shots at the Germans which resumed the war. The following Christmas, the soldiers were warned, in advance, that they would be court martialed for sharing such holiday cheer with the enemy.

Historians disagree on key factors of the origins of this war that left an estimated 17 million dead and 20 million wounded. Did these soldiers even know why they were fighting? Like Murdoch Wood said, if they had been left to themselves, there would never have been another shot fired.

REFLECTIONS

Fast forward again to more recent history. Meddling from another country, through social media, has convinced millions of people to take stances that are based on lies and propaganda. Propaganda is not new. It worked in the 1930s through print, radio, and film, much to the delight of Hitler and Goebbels. Today, however, the hate-fueling effects of propaganda are accelerated by social media. It is now widely known that Russian forces, interested in dividing the United States of America and influencing the 2016 presidential election, opened thousands of fake social media accounts, spent over $100,000 in ads, and even usurped names of actual groups to reach targeted audiences. In one example, a Facebook page they called "Heart of Texas," which attracted people to the messaging "Stop the Islamization of Texas," and another page for which they usurped the name of an actual group, "The United Muslims of America," the Russian imposters provoked a protest and counter-protest at the Islamic Da'Wa Center in Houston. Law enforcement was brought in when the situation escalated to the point of someone calling for the "need to blow this place up." Without this interference from others, these people would have most likely stayed home and not thought much about stoking the fires of hate. This kind of damage takes years, if not generations, to undo. This is one example of many throughout the years, and there will be many more if we aren't more careful than we have been.

It seems we have not evolved at all since 1731 and the travails of John Francis Wade. He, and many like him, fled England because of a dangerous atmosphere of fear, anger, and hate set in motion by whom? By a religious leader who wanted government control, and government leaders who wanted religious control. And the masses were duped into division.

Since my children were in grade school, I've repeated (ad nauseam, they would probably say), "If you look for the good in something or someone, I promise you, you will find it. If you look for the bad, I promise you, you will find it." What is it that draws so many of us to put more emphasis on what people have done wrong than what they have done that's good and life-affirming?

I never would've thought that looking deeper into Christmas carols would have led me to study trench warfare and "Holy War." But here I am, asking this question: What voices are we listening to? Are those voices based in love or hate? How often are we called to step out of our safety zones and

What voices are we listening to?

show love to people, but instead we stay cramped down in trenches dug by history, society, traditions, misunderstandings, coliseum mentality, and plain, old-fashioned fear? Can we recognize that it is not God inciting these wars, but rather an evil force outside of ourselves, lying to us, laughing as it pulls our focus away from our true purpose: to love God's people here on earth. If we look for the good in others, we will find it. If we listen for those voices, really listen, we will realize that there are musical strains reaching toward us from the "enemy camps," notes of acceptance, tones of tolerance, peaceful pitches inviting us to blend our voices with theirs to strike chords of understanding. A cappella. Unaccompanied by instruments of division.

When we blend our voices together in caroling, the common language of music builds bridges of harmony between even the deadliest of enemies.

CHAPTER 7

O Little Town of Bethlehem

The Hopes and Fears of All the Years

O Little Town of Bethlehem
How still we see thee lie.
Above thy deep and dreamless sleep
The silent stars go by.
Yet in thy dark streets shineth
The everlasting light!
The hopes and fears of all the years
Are met in thee tonight.

For Christ is born of Mary
And gathered all above.

While mortals sleep the angels keep
Their watch of wondering love.
O morning stars together
Proclaim the holy birth,
And praises sing to God the King
And peace to men on earth.

How silently, how silently
The wondrous gift is given.
So God imparts to human hearts
The blessings of His heaven.
No ear may hear His coming,
But in this world of sin,
Where meek souls will receive him still
The dear Christ enters in.

Where children pure and happy
Pray to the blessed Child,
Where misery cries out to Thee,
Son of the mother mild;
Where charity stands watching
And faith holds wide the door,
the dark night wakes, the glory breaks,
And Christmas comes once more.

O holy Child of Bethlehem
Descend to us, we pray.
Cast out our sin and enter in
Be born to us today.
We hear the Christmas angels
The great glad tidings tell
O come to us, abide with us
Our Lord Emmanuel.

Year written: 1868
Words: Phillips Brooks (1835–1893)
Music: Lewis H. Redner (1831–1908)

These beautiful verses (one of which I hadn't seen before, but I find to be more beautiful than the more famous verses) were written by Phillips Brooks in 1868. You may have heard of the Phillips Brooks School in Menlo Park, California, known for its small class sizes and excellent reputation for a grade school. It was named after this same Phillips Brooks. Brooks once dreamt of being a Latin teacher. He studied at Harvard and went on to teach at the Boston Latin School, but he became very discouraged, feeling that he'd failed at his vocation. He turned to prayer and bible study and then went back to school to become a Christian minister. He was ordained in 1860, and two years after starting his ministry, he found himself commissioned as the pastor of the Holy Trinity Church in Philadelphia with a reputation as a great orator. His spirit-filled messages increased the membership of his church to standing room only, and his talents became known far and wide.

But an immense, dark canopy was draping over the nation, concealing brotherly love and robbing American congregations everywhere of their spirit. The Civil War, which began the year before Brooks stepped into the pulpit at Holy Trinity, raged on for the next four years. Brooks saw the grief and punctured hopes of his beloved congregation, and he wanted to lift them. He preached valiantly, but it was a difficult undertaking, as his spirit was suffering the same blows. When the war finally ended in 1865, he thought the healing would begin. Then the unthinkable happened. Their dear president Lincoln, to whom so much of the nation looked for pure-hearted wisdom, was assassinated. The president who famously said, "Be sure to put your feet in the right place, and then stand firm," had been knocked off of his feet only in death.

Phillips Brooks, the pastor with the reputation for such moving oratory skills, was called upon to give a speech he never wanted nor dreamed of giving. He spoke at President Lincoln's funeral. His grief, admiration for Lincoln, acknowledgment of the evils that had caused the country to be where it found itself, and a call to action for Americans to hold themselves to a higher standard are all poignantly on display in that speech.

One brave, reckless man came forth to cast himself, almost single-handedly, with a hopeless hope, against the proud power that he hated, and trust to the influence of a soul marching on into the history of his countrymen to stir them to a vindication of the truth he loved;...that swarthy multitudes came in, ragged, and tired, and hungry, and ignorant, but free forever from anything but the memorial scars of the fetters and the whip, singing rude songs in which the new triumph of freedom struggled and heaved below the sad melody that had been shaped for bondage...But slavery will not die...while one man counts another man his born inferior for the color of his skin...So let him lie here in our midst today...this best and most American of all Americans...May God make us worthy of the memory of Abraham Lincoln!

How did the man who wrote these stinging words restore his spirit enough to pen the sweet lullaby "O Little Town of Bethlehem?" It didn't happen right away. Brooks was beyond weary and his spirit was broken. He needed a respite for his soul; to take a break and reacquaint himself with the goodness of the Lord in a place far away from the shell-shocked land in which he felt the weight of grief and disillusionment like a great boulder on his shoulders.

Brooks went on a pilgrimage to the Holy Land. He would write in his journal about how inspired he was during his visit. His journal entries include his account of visiting the very land where it is said the shepherds were watching their flocks when the angels appeared to them and heralded the birth of the Savior. He was touched to see that there were still shepherds there at the time of his visit, watching their flocks. It took his breath away to hear the hymns of praise being sung in the church near the spot where it is believed Jesus was born. In this place, Brooks was able to deeply inhale God's love. He felt full of the Holy Spirit once again and was eager to convey his experience to his congregation so as to lift them up and bridge the gap between despair and hope for them.

When he returned from his sabbatical, he jumped right in with renewed vigor, describing the images, feelings, and inspirations he received in Bethlehem, but his words and enthusiasm were failing him. His congregation didn't seem to be able to open their wounded, bandaged hearts to take the breath of the fresh air their pastor was offering them. He tried, week after week and month after month, for over two years. He felt as though he was, once again, pushing that heavy boulder uphill. Even his friend, Lewis Redner, whom he'd hired to be the church organist his first year at Holy Trinity, couldn't seem to grasp the spiritual uplift Brooks was trying, with all of his might, to convey.

As Brooks looked ahead toward the preparations he would need to make for the Christmas service of 1868, he also looked back at his treasured time in Bethlehem. He began to relive it in his mind, writing it down as a poem. He gave it to Redner and asked him to put it to music for their Christmas Sunday service.

Reading Brook's poem, Redner finally understood the powerful feelings Brooks had been trying to convey. He was so moved that he wanted to write a grand, majestic melody with which to do Brook's poem justice, but he couldn't seem to do it. He struggled and struggled right up until Christmas Eve, and then went to bed, feeling as though he'd failed. In the middle of the night, a melody came to him in a dream. This melody wasn't anything like

Reading Brook's poem, Redner finally understood the powerful feelings Brooks had been trying to convey.

what he was trying to create for Brook's words, but it was so clear and persistent that he woke up, got out of bed, and went to the poem. He applied the melody, and it fit Brook's words perfectly! On that Christmas Sunday, the children of Philadelphia's Holy Trinity Church sang "O Little Town of Bethlehem," playing a vital part in the post–Civil War healing in that community. Some of their worst fears had already visited them and broken their spirits. Now an old friend came tapping on their hearts—their Christmas spirit—with renewed meaning. Within the Philadelphia city limits, with their hearts opened to the spirit Brooks had been trying to infuse in them, they found a new zest in their hopes, which met with and overcame their fears through the gift of a Savior, born in a quiet, little town.

REFLECTIONS

As I consider each carol, I often start out by simply looking more deeply into the meaning of the lyrics. As a caroler, I have always tried to be very present and conscious of what I'm communicating when I'm caroling, but, if I'm being very honest, I have to admit that these lyrics I've been singing—some of them since childhood—do sometimes roll off my tongue too easily.

I'm guessing that anyone who grew up celebrating Christmas knows the first verse to "O Little Town of Bethlehem." It's as sweet as a lullaby. It conjures a beautiful Christmas Eve scene. We get images of a sleepy, rural setting at night—it's dark, it's quiet, the sky is peppered with stars. Everyone is asleep. Jesus is born there. And the rest is just pretty language. Fa la lah! It's easy to sing it without thinking about it. But then I took a more personal look at those words.

O Little Town of Bethlehem

It's a little town famous for nothing at that time. Probably pretty boring, and slow paced.

When I was growing up, my family took a trip out west. It was a big summer vacation for which my stepdad, Ed, built a luggage box to secure to the top of our red station wagon. My brother, sister, two step-brothers, mom, and I filled the seats and Dad took the wheel and drove us from Michigan to places like Mt. Rushmore and Yellowstone Park. After one particularly long day of driving, we were getting drowsy in Nebraska, and as it got about time to find a motel, we went through town after town looking for a room, but there was nothing available. We even tried the hotels! Nothing! It was getting very late, and we were all tired and needed to go to sleep. We were getting kind of worried when we found this tiny, one inter-section town and an old motel, which looked about as pooped as we felt. We were so relieved when Dad came back to the car with room keys! We slept two and three to a bed that night. The mattresses were so old, they dipped down in the middle, and we kept falling into each other all night. This town was called Lodgepole. I'll never forget it. So, I imagined:

Oh "Lodgepole," you little, obscure, slow, quiet (except for the train that wakes us up every hour) town . . .

Above Thy Deep And Dreamless Sleep The Silent Stars Go By

Deep and dreamless sleep.

The people of this town, as with Bethlehem, are laborers. They work hard, long hours, and they are

tired! Too tired for restless sleep. Too tired to notice
if they fall into the middle of the mattress. Too tired
to hear the trains passing by. Too tired for dreams. Or
if they do dream, they are sleeping so hard, they don't
remember them. Yet, the very same silent stars going
by Bethlehem also go by Lodgepole—as my friend,
Mark, recently pointed out—providing a universal
connection for all of us, up above, if only we look up
and appreciate it. The fact that the stars are always
above us reaffirms, in his mind, that we are more alike
than different. I like that.

Yet in Thy Dark Streets Shineth the Everlasting Light!

Imagine if Christ had been born in Lodgepole,
Nebraska. Little town, you are dark right now but
inside your limits, the light of the world is being born!
Inside YOU!

The Hopes and Fears of All the Years Are Met in Thee Tonight

The hopes and fears of *all* the years: all of the years
that were, that are, and that will ever be—*all* the years.

What are those hopes? That we are pleasing to
God? That we are able to have children? That they
grow up to be healthy, happy, good people who make
a positive difference in this world? That we are safe?

That we are prosperous? That there is a heaven to welcome us when we leave this earth? That there will finally be peace on earth?

What are those fears? Illness? Pain? Poverty? Heartache? Hell? War breaking out, stealing our peace and visiting injury and loss upon us?

This verse is saying that the hopes and the fears *meet* when this precious Gift, sent from God, is present among us, to show us that God loves us more than we could ever imagine, and to show us how to pray, how to strive to live, how to love, and that we are stronger and more important in the eyes of Heaven than we could ever know. And that if we focus on Him and follow His example, we will not die and go to hell or die and have nothingness. But that we will, indeed, go to heaven and live in the presence of God. These are some of the perennial hopes and fears of the people of Bethlehem, Lodgepole, the very places where we find ourselves right now, and the people in the pews of the post-Civil War Holy Trinity Church of Philadelphia. Like them, perhaps some of our worst fears have already visited us and threaten to break our spirits. Can we open our hearts to the spirit Phillips Brooks infused into this carol? If we will try, then we are likely to find new meaning in our hopes, as we allow them to calm our fears through the gift of a Savior, born in a quiet, little town.

CHAPTER 8

I Heard the Bells on Christmas Day

**It was as if an earthquake rent the
hearthstones of a continent**

I Heard the Bells on Christmas Day
Their old, familiar carols play,
    And wild and sweet
    The words repeat
Of peace on earth, good-will to men!

I thought how as the day had come
The belfries of all Christendom
    Had rolled along

The unbroken song
Of peace on earth, good-will to men!

Then in despair I bowed my head;
"There is no peace on earth" I said;
    "For hate is strong
    And mocks the song
Of peace on earth, good-will to men!"

Then pealed the bells more loud and deep
God is not dead, nor doth He sleep
    The wrong shall fail
    The right prevail
With peace on earth, good-will to men!

Till ringing, singing on its way,
The world revolved from night to day,
    A voice, a chime,
    A chant sublime
Of peace on earth, good-will to men!

Words: Henry Wadsworth Longfellow (1807–1882)
Music: John Baptiste Calkin (1827–1905)

For many years of my caroling career (especially since September 11, 2001), I understood this carol to be one that resonated with people who were in pain, so the day I set out to learn more about its history was one of revelation to me. It made so much sense to read that its wordsmith, Henry Wadsworth Longfellow, a revered American poet (1807–1882), penned these words out of a broken heart. After his first wife, whom he loved very much and with whom he was very happy, died at a young age, he needed significant time to mourn. After seven years, he remarried. They had five children and for years he was happy again until she tragically died in a horrific accident. Longfellow was still grieving her death when the Civil War began, and his sorrow was compounded. A man of faith, he believed in a strong God and the power of prayer. He pleaded with God to bring an end to the fighting and discord in his country.

His oldest son, Charles, was 19 years old and a soldier in the war when he was badly injured and sent home to convalesce. As Henry tended to Charles, his anger and despair overtook his prayers. He saw many people in their hometown of Cambridge, Massachusetts who were badly injured soldiers or who had lost their soldier sons in the war. He directed his rage and incredulity toward his craft.

The title for the poem that would become "I Heard the Bells on Christmas Day" was "Christmas Bells." He wrote it on Christmas Day, 1863. I can imagine him listening to the Christmas bells ringing out all over Cambridge inspiring him to pick up his pen. There are verses that I'd never seen or heard that were left out of the song, presumably because they are darkly focused on the Civil War and not of the spirit we most associate with the holy day. Even with these verses removed, some darkness remains, but with a slight rearrangement of the remaining verses, this carol reflects that there is darkness in the world, but that it will not overcome the light, and the song ends on a triumphant note.

CHRISTMAS BELLS

I Heard the Bells on Christmas Day
Their old, familiar carols play,
 And wild and sweet
 The words repeat
Of peace on earth, good-will to men!

And thought how as the day had come
The belfries of all Christendom
 Had rolled along
 The unbroken song
Of peace on earth, good-will to men!

Till ringing, singing on it's way,
The world revolved from night to day,
 A voice, a chime,
 A chant sublime
Of peace on earth, good-will to men!

Then from each black, accursed mouth
The cannon thundered in the South,
 And with the sound
 The carols drowned
Of peace on earth, good-will to men!

It was as if an earthquake rent
The hearthstones of a continent,
 And made forlorn

The households born
Of peace on earth, good-will to men!

Then in despair I bowed my head;
"There is no peace on earth" I said;
      "For hate is strong
      And mocks the song
Of peace on earth, good-will to men!"

Then pealed the bells more loud and deep
God is not dead, nor doth He sleep
      The wrong shall fail
      The right prevail
With peace on earth, good-will to men!

Written: December 25, 1863
Henry Wadsworth Longfellow (1807–1882)

REFLECTION

I have long considered "I Heard the Bells on Christmas Day" to be the most poignant of all of the carols. When I look back over my 20+ years of caroling with I SMILE, there are some memories that stand out more than others. One dates way back to 1998, but it stands out as clearly as if it were yesterday.

A trio of us were caroling at a big department store in Manhattan. It was a week before Christmas. We were happy to add to the gaiety of the general atmosphere, although most of the shoppers passed us by, mission-minded and at hyper velocities. Midway through one carol, I noticed a store employee watching us, expectantly, as though he was eager to make a request. We finished the carol and turned to him. He did have a request, but it wasn't for a carol.

He told us he worked in the makeup department, and that they had a long-time, regular client who came in every day, and sat at the counter and talked with the staff. His eyes were kind and almost pleading as he told us that he was sure that this woman would truly enjoy our coming over and caroling for her. It was easy to see that this client's visits to his counter had caused him to care about her and that he wanted to bring her some joy.

We were happy to oblige. He led us to the makeup department and to his counter where we found her seated, and he introduced us to her. She was an elderly lady, dressed impeccably, with coiffed hair and tasteful makeup. She was of the generation to whom dressing up was part of the fun of going shopping. She smiled at us, but her drooped shoulders and eyes, which looked up at us past her brows, belied a sadness. Her eyes seemed unconnected to her smile. A woman her age has probably seen a lot of loss. Perhaps even recently.

We asked her if there was a carol she'd like to hear.

"Oh, yes! That'd be lovely," she replied.

"Something cheerful?" we suggested. "'Deck the Halls'? 'Have a Holly Jolly Christmas'?"

"No...," she trailed, looking for the right words. "You know what I need? I need something I can cry to."

Something to cry to. I understood. A few years earlier, harboring pangs of a lingering broken heart, but feeling too foolish to share my pain with anyone, I found myself having a glass of wine at an elegant, old New York City tavern. This establishment had an atmosphere of dark woodwork, dim lighting, and achingly mournful music. Billie Holiday was playing. Perfect. It felt not only allowable, but appropriate to let a tear or two escape. I did. And it felt so good—an unexpected relief. In that moment, I learned that music is a blessing not only when it lifts our spirits, but also when it releases the protective grip we hold on our hearts and sets free the tears we need to experience.

In that moment, I learned that music is a blessing not only when it lifts our spirits, but also when it releases the protective grip we hold on our hearts and sets free the tears we need to experience.

"Something to cry to. I know just the thing." I said.

We turned to "I Heard the Bells on Christmas Day." We started in on the slow, thoughtful first verses, then picked up the volume and tempo for the angry, accusatory third verse, then slipped in the hope of the fourth, and the quiet celebration of the fifth verse. She cried. Then she smiled a smile that *was* connected to her shining eyes.

"Thank you. That was exactly what I needed."

Since that time, I've noticed greater appreciation for that carol, during times when our spirits are ailing, like right after 9/11, and any time we are shaken to the core at the inhumanity we are seeing in the news or all around us every day. It may feel like an earthquake has rent the hearthstones of our continent. It may feel like the hatred we hear threatens to drown out the carols of Christmas, but Christmas spirit is alive in carols, and as with "I Heard the Bells on Christmas Day" and others, the carols of Christmas have proven, through the years, that they have the power to drown out the hate!

CHAPTER 9

The Twelve Days of Christmas

When You Walk with God, the Gifts of the Spirit Move in Your Life as Easily as a Swan on Water

On the first day of Christmas, my true love gave to me
    A partridge in a pear tree.

On the second day of Christmas, my true love gave to me
    Two French hens,
    And a partridge in a pear tree.

On the third day of Christmas, my true love gave to me

Three French hens,
Two turtle doves,
And a partridge in a pear tree.

On the fourth day of Christmas, my true love gave to me
Four calling birds,
Three French hens,
Two turtle doves,
And a partridge in a pear tree.

On the fifth day of Christmas, my true love gave to me
Five golden rings,
Four calling birds,
Three French hens,
Two turtle doves,
And a partridge in a pear tree.

On the sixth day of Christmas, my true love gave to me
Six geese a'laying,
Five golden rings,
Four calling birds,
Three French hens,
Two turtle doves,
And a partridge in a pear tree.

On the seventh day of Christmas, my true love gave to me
Seven swans a'swimming,
Six geese a'laying,
Five golden rings,
Four calling birds,
Three French hens,
Two turtle doves,
And a partridge in a pear tree.

On the eighth day of Christmas, my true love gave to me

Eight maids a'milking,
Seven swans a'swimming,
Six geese a'laying,
Five golden rings,
Four calling birds,
Three French hens,
Two turtle doves,
And a partridge in a pear tree.

On the ninth day of Christmas, my true love gave to me
Nine ladies dancing,
Eight maids a'milking,
Seven swans a'swimming,
Six geese a'laying,
Five golden rings,
Four calling birds,
Three French hens,
Two turtle doves,
And a partridge in a pear tree.

On the tenth day of Christmas, my true love gave to me
Ten lords a'leaping,
Nine ladies dancing,
Eight maids a'milking,
Seven swans a'swimming,
Six geese a'laying,
Five golden rings,
Four calling birds,
Three French hens,
Two turtle doves,
And a partridge in a pear tree.

On the eleventh day of Christmas, my true love gave to me
Eleven pipers piping,

Ten lords a'leaping,
Nine ladies dancing,
Eight maids a'milking,
Seven swans a'swimming,
Six geese a'laying,
Five golden rings,
Four calling birds,
Three French hens,
Two turtle doves,
And a partridge in a pear tree.

On the twelfth day of Christmas, my true love gave to me
Twelve drummers drumming,
Eleven pipers piping,
Ten lords a'leaping,
Nine ladies dancing,
Eight maids a'milking,
Seven swans a'swimming,
Six geese a'laying,
Five golden rings,
Four calling birds,
Three French hens,
Two turtle doves,
And a partridge in a pear tree.

Origins unknown
First printed: 1780 in the *Mirth Without Mischief,* children's book

Have you ever asked yourself what "The Twelve Days of Christmas" is all about? Doesn't it seem nonsensical? What does this cacophony of birds, entertainers, laborers, and jewelry have to do with Christmas, anyway? Sleuthing out the origins of

"The Twelve Days of Christmas" leads us to a story of intrigue, danger, and mystery! Legend has it that the song was written to teach 16th century English children the tenets of Catholicism at a time when Roman Catholics had to go underground to practice or teach their faith. Could it be that it was one of the most successful secret codes of all time?

Here and there in my journey through the carols, I've been excited to read about a fascinating back-story of a particular carol, and then later find that it is disputed. The legend of "The Twelve Days of Christmas" being a secret code has its detractors. The accounts I've read that try to disprove the idea do not actually disprove it. The strongest refutation they are able to present is that the legend cannot be proven. Some Roman Catholic scholars and church historians agree that the origins of this seemingly silly carol are actually based in a shroud of secret oral catechism, used to teach the Roman Catholic faith at a time when the practice and teaching of the faith were forbidden and punishable by imprisonment and even death.

When I was in grade school, our music teacher Mrs. Dabney had us memorize a song called "Fifty-Nifty United States," which lists all 50 states in alphabetic order. I can still recite them, with the melody of the song running through my mind in 23 seconds! Thank you, Mrs. Dabney! That has come in so very handy throughout my life that I wish I had watched more Schoolhouse Rock when I was a child. If I had, I'd be able to tell you how a bill becomes a law, and so many other topics that didn't come naturally for me. My point is that learning is tremendously enhanced when the subject is put to music and the words capture our imagination. Therefore, I think this would have been a brilliant and fun way to teach difficult ideas to children. Even if this mysterious account of the origins of the carol were to be disproven, it can still act as a tool for learning parts of the bible and catechism today.

Here is the symbolism hidden behind the cast of characters:

On the First Day of Christmas, My True Love Gave to Me

First, we need to ask, "Who is my true love?" Our true love is God. Our truest love, you could say.

A Partridge in a Pear Tree

The partridge is Jesus! Some say that the tree represents the cross. When I delved deeper, I learned that Christ is symbolically represented as a mother partridge, which is the only hen that feigns injury to decoy predators from her helpless nestlings, which recalls Christ's sadness over the fate of Jerusalem. As he says (Luke 13:34), "Jerusalem! Jerusalem!... How often would I have sheltered you under my wings, as a hen does her chicks, but you would not have it so."

On the Second Day of Christmas, My True Love Gave to Me: Two Turtledoves

The two turtledoves are the old and the new testaments.

On the Third Day of Christmas, My True Love Gave to Me: Three French Hens

The three French hens are faith, hope, and love, from 1 Corinthians 13:13.

On the Fourth Day of Christmas, My True Love Gave to Me: Four Calling Birds

The four calling birds are the gospels of Matthew, Mark, Luke, and John.

On the Fifth Day of Christmas My True Love Gave to Me: Five Golden Rings!

The five golden rings represent the first five books of the Torah—the Books of Moses:

1. Genesis, Bereshit, "In the beginning"
2. Exodus, Shemot, "Names"
3. Leviticus, Vayikra, "And He called"

4. Numbers, Bemidbar, "In the wilderness"
5. Deuteronomy, Devarim, "Words"

On the Sixth Day of Christmas, My True Love Gave to Me: Six Geese A'laying

The six geese represent the six days of creation.

On the Seventh Day of Christmas, My True Love Gave to Me: Seven Swans A'swimming

The seven swans a'swimming represent the seven gifts of the Holy Spirit:

1. Wisdom
2. Understanding
3. Counsel
4. Fortitude
5. Knowledge
6. Piety
7. Fear of the Lord

We are taught, through this legend, that when you walk with God, the gifts of the spirit move in your life as easily as a swan on water. Isn't that beautiful?

On the Eighth Day of Christmas, My True Love Gave to Me: Eight Maids A'milking

The eight maids a'milking represent the eight

beatitudes from Jesus' Sermon on the Mount, from the Gospel of Matthew 5:3-12:

1. Blessed are the poor in spirit
2. Those who mourn
3. The meek
4. Those who hunger and thirst for righteousness
5. The merciful
6. The pure in heart
7. The peacemakers
8. Those who are persecuted for righteousness' sake

On the Ninth Day of Christmas, My True Love Gave to Me: Nine Ladies Dancing

The nine ladies dancing are the nine "fruits" of the Holy Spirit. Catholic Catechism says that "The fruits of the Spirit are perfections that the Holy Spirit forms in us as the first fruits of eternal glory" (Galatians 22–23). Again, I had no recollection of these, but I like the idea that there are the seven gifts of the Holy Spirit, and then the nine fruits of those gifts. And lovely gifts they are, too:

1. Love
2. Joy
3. Peace
4. Patience

5. Kindness
6. Generosity
7. Faithfulness
8. Gentleness
9. Self-control

On the Tenth Day of Christmas, My True Love Gave to Me: Ten Lords A'leaping

The lords a'leaping are the 10 Commandments. I was about to make the assumption that I didn't need to bother with this famous list, but then I thought, *A refresher couldn't hurt*. Here is the barebones list. For the full content, see Exodus 20:2-17.

1. You shall have no other gods before Me.
2. You shall not make for yourself an idol in the shape of anything.
3. You shall not take the name of the Lord your God in vain.
4. Remember the Sabbath day, by keeping it holy.
5. Honor your father and your mother.
6. You shall not murder.
7. You shall not commit adultery.
8. You shall not steal.
9. You shall not bear false witness against your neighbor.
10. You shall not covet your neighbor's house, wife or property.

On the Eleventh Day of Christmas, My True Love Gave to Me: Eleven Pipers Piping

The 11 pipers are the 11 *faithful* disciples of Christ: Simon Peter, Andrew, James, John, Philip, Thomas, Matthew, James, Thaddeus, Simon, and Bartholomew.

Obviously, Judas did not make the cut.

On the Twelfth Day of Christmas, My True Love Gave to Me: Twelve Drummers Drumming

I guess they wanted to "drum" the 12 points of the Apostle's Creed into those young heads:

1. I believe in God, the Father almighty, Creator of heaven and earth.
2. I believe in Jesus Christ, His only Son, our Lord.
3. He was conceived by the power of the Holy Spirit and born of the virgin Mary.
4. He suffered under Pontius Pilate, was crucified, died, and was buried. He descended into hell.
5. On the third day, he rose again. He ascended into heaven and is seated at the right hand of the Father.
6. He will come again to judge the living and the dead.
7. I believe in the Holy Spirit,
8. the holy Catholic church,
9. the communion of saints,

10. the forgiveness of sins,
11. the resurrection of the body,
12. and life everlasting. Amen.

REFLECTIONS

When I take the time to really consider the legendary symbolism, I find myself surprisingly enriched! For instance, when I studied the seven swans, so beautifully representing the gifts of the Holy Spirit, I learned that these gifts are virtues that originally appeared in the book of Isaiah 11:1–2. I was surprised to learn that in the Hebrew translation there are six virtues and in the Greek there are seven. I looked to see which one is missing from the Hebrew: piety. I never liked that word. It has always struck me as "holier than thou," as we say. It calls to my mind examples of people who take too much pride in being "religious" rather than having actual compassion for people. Merriam-Webster defines it with words like "obligations" and "dutifulness in religion." So, I looked up some other definitions and—lo and behold—I've decided that I have changed my mind about the word. (Isn't it nice to discover anew that we are able to change our minds?)

Now my idea of piety has everything to do with reverence and spiritual devotion. A person with reverence recognizes their reliance on God and has a mindset of trust, love, and humility in relation to God. I asked myself if this is something that I want to do without. My answer is, "No way!" There are many nights when I know I could not get to sleep if this was not my reality. Pope Francis said that piety reminds us that we belong to God, that we have a deep bond with God, and that this relationship gives meaning to our whole life, even during the most troubled moments. He said,

> "Piety is not mere outward religiosity; it is that genuine . . . spirit that makes us...grow in love for others, seeing them as our brothers and sisters, . . ."

I like that. My spirit is refreshed to be more aware of this virtue and to have made a conscious decision about it. That wouldn't have happened if I hadn't taken the time to study this seemingly silly carol.

CHAPTER 10

Here We Come A-Wassailing

THE WASSAIL SONG
(GLOUCESTERSHIRE'S WASSAILING SONG)

Wassail, Wassail all over the town!
Our toast it is white and our ale it is brown.
Our bowl, it is made of the White Maple Tree
With our wassailing bowl we'll drink to thee!

And here's to Cherry and to his right eye,
Pray God send our master a good piece of pie!
And a good piece of pie, that may we all see
With our wassailing bowl we'll drink to thee!

Come butler, come fill us a bowl of the best

Then we hope that your soul in heaven may rest.
But if you do draw us a bowl of the small
Then down shall go butler, bowl and all.

Be here any maids? I suppose there be some;
Sure they will not let young men stand on the cold stone!
Sing Hey O! Maids, come trole back the pin,
And the fairest maid in the house let us all in.

HERE WE COME A-WASSAILING

Here we come a-wassailing among the leaves so green!
Here we come a-wandring so fair to be seen!

Refrain:
Love and joy come to you, and to you your wassail too
And God bless you and send you a happy new year
And God send you a happy new year.

We are not daily beggars that beg from door to door,
But we are neighbors' children whom you have
        seen before.

Refrain

Good master and good mistress,
As you sit beside the fire,
Pray think of us poor children
Who wander in the mire.

Refrain

We have a little purse
Made of ratching leather skin;
We want some of your small change
To line it well within.

Refrain

God bless the master of this house, likewise the mistress too,
And all the little children that round the table go!

Refrain

And all your kin and kinsfolk that dwell both far and near,
We wish a merry Christmas and happy new year!

Refrain

WE WISH YOU A MERRY CHRISTMAS

We Wish You a Merry Christmas
We Wish You a Merry Christmas
We Wish You a Merry Christmas
And a happy new year.

Refrain:
Good tidings we bring to you and your kin,
Good tiding for Christmas and a happy new year!

Now bring us some figgy pudding
Now bring us some figgy pudding
Now bring us some figgy pudding
And a cup of good cheer!

Refrain

For we all love figgy pudding
For we all love figgy pudding
For we all love figgy pudding
So bring some out here!

Refrain

And we won't go until we get some
And we won't go until we get some
And we won't go until we get some
So bring some out here!

Refrain

Thought to have originated as early
as the 5th to the 15th centuries
England

No, this is not a misprint. This chapter is about three carols because they are all songs that were, historically, sung by wassailers and served the same unique purpose. In modern times, wassail is pronounced in two different ways: wä-səl *also* wä-ˈsāl. Wassailer is pronounced: wä-sə-lər *also* wä-ˈsā-lər. Whichever feels best to you, go for it. I tend to lean toward the first pronunciation, because when we sing the words in "Here We Come A-Wassailing," the accent is on the first syllable, musically speaking, and this is the more common wassail song. In fact, for years, it was the only one that I had known and that my carolers sang. However, in "The Wassail Song," which originates from the county of Gloucestershire, and is often referred to as "Gloucestershire's Wassailing Song," the musical accent is on the second syllable. When speaking the words, my feeling is that it takes a little less energy to put the accent on the first syllable, and so it flows off the tongue more easily. But that's just me. You decide for yourself.

So, what the heck is wassail, who were the wassailers, and what is wassailing you may be wondering? Wassailers were precursors to carolers, and wassailing was the first form of door-to-door Christmas caroling, but shockingly, it has a dangerous and desperate past. The word derives from a Middle English greeting: "Waes Hael" meant "Be in Good Health." Originally, the *w* was pronounced as a *v*. The original custom was that of someone holding up a glass and toasting a person's health by saying "Waes Hael" and then taking a sip. The proper response was then for the recipient of the toast to take a sip from their cup after saying "Drink Hael!" The beverage itself was also called wassail, and usually consisted of any variety of combinations of spiced beer, mead, wine, or cider, with or without fruit bobbing about in it, and served from a wassail bowl. So, wassail is both a salutation and a festive beverage for toasting one's health.

In the hundreds of years leading up to and including the Victorian Era, in England, there was a great divide between the rich and poor. As is well-chronicled in many of the works of Charles Dickens and elsewhere, the wealthy of England controlled the money and the law of the land. Furthermore, the people who wrote the laws were not interested in taking care of the poor among them. The people who were well-off tended to think of poverty as a moral defect. Therefore, if one was born poor, there was almost nothing that person could do to change their status, short of being some sort of a genius like Dickens himself, who suffered the horrors of workhouse child labor while his family was in debtor's prison. Christmastime, however, as Scrooge's nephew Fred pointed out, was a time when people seemed to "open their shut-up hearts freely, and to think of people below them."

The people who were well-off tended to think of poverty as a moral defect.

Taking advantage of this annual, charitable state of consciousness could have meant the difference between life and death for the most meager among them. Therefore, the poor wassailers, often farm laborers or their children (the children tended to yield better results, probably because they more naturally pulled on heartstrings) went door-to-door at Christmastime. They sang—or wassailed—for their wealthier neighbors and offered them a cup of Christmas cheer from a decorated wassail bowl, hoping for some charitable gesture in return. The bowl itself was commonly made of maple or syca-more wood and was usually the bowl used to serve boiled potatoes at the farm family's dinner table. The wassailers would decorate the bowl with greenery and ribbons in hopes that their festive efforts would evoke such tenderness from their hosts as to fetch a gratuity of food, drink, or coins. Indeed, after trudging through the wind and snow in their pitifully scant garments, these wassailers were often welcomed into the homes to warm up, have some holiday refreshments, and sometimes given a coin that provided some measure of desperately needed relief.

As the centuries passed, the tradition of the poverty-ravished children wassailing morphed into scenes of brazen, drunken bullies stumbling door-to-door. They had no cheer to offer by way of a wassail bowl, but, instead, they improvised verses of wassail songs, bellowing out their rude demands. The verses at the top of the chapter are just a sampling of the countless hooliganisms and rogueries that became the trend. They had many demands, ranging from the famous figgy pudding and alcoholic drinks to household items. Indecent overtures were even howled out to the maidens of the house. The holiday looked more like what we know as modern day celebrations of Halloween, Mardi Gras, or St. Patrick's Day than Christmas: excessive drinking, doors being broken down, fist fights breaking out, rape, and even murder!

In some areas of England and in colonial New

England, the police were on high alert from Christmas Eve until New Year's Eve. The seasonal marauding and the thought of the impending danger at their very door steps repulsed and terrorized respectable citizens and the holiday was largely blackened for them. The Puritans of England, after overthrowing King Charles I and having him beheaded in 1647, formally banned Christmas. Parliament decreed that fasting and humiliation for Englishmen to account for their sins should be the order of the day on December 25. The Puritans in New England followed suit, and businesses stayed open and church doors closed on December 25. The colony at Massachusetts Bay made it a criminal offense to publicly celebrate Christmas, punishable by a 5 shilling fine. In 1660 the monarchy was restored, and it was once again legal to celebrate Christmas publicly in England. Massachusetts, however, held firm to its ban for many more years. Under the reign of King Charles II, the pressure for Massachusetts to relax its unnecessarily stringent laws mounted, with a threat of revoking the colony's royal charter. In 1681, the colony repealed its ban on Christmas. By this time,

The colony at Massachusetts Bay made it a criminal offense to publicly celebrate Christmas, punishable by a 5 shilling fine.

the offending tradition seems to have been forgotten, and the wassailing thugs no longer posed a threat.

REFLECTIONS

I wonder, *how did the humble tradition of inviting charity with gifts of drink, song, and toasting the health of prosperous neighbors turn into such miscreant perverseness?* Did the boys who were once such cold, hungry little waifs, so grateful for a coin, feel the heavy thumb of the wealthy on them as they grew up? Did they grow increasingly aware of their powerlessness to change their status in life? Did they develop bulky muscles, laboring long, hard hours without recognition or advancement as grown men? And then, during those few days of the year when they felt recognized, did they embolden themselves with alcohol and use their might to punish the people they blamed for keeping them in such desperate straits?

When the Wassail songs led me to read about how, in Victorian England and earlier, the upper class looked upon poverty as a defect and that they had little interest in helping the poor, I found myself stunned anew by the cruelty and willful ignorance of such a mindset. This was not the mindset of just one Scrooge, but it was the accepted practice of a large and powerful enough conglomerate to keep a whole class of people down and suffering for generations. I had been aware of this chasm of the classes since at least since the 11th grade when I performed in my school's musical production of *OLIVER!* which is based on Charles Dicken's novel about the orphan Oliver Twist. But it was easy—it still *is* easy—to think, "Well, that's just the way things were back then. They didn't really know much better, did they? *Now* we are so much more evolved. That kind of thing doesn't really happen anymore, and certainly not in the United States of America!"

But are we that much more evolved? Once again, I find myself amazed that Christmas carols have me studying something as seemingly unrelated as modern socioeconomics! But now that I'm looking

Right here, in my own American backyard, it seems to me that we are trending back to a similar dynamic as in Victorian England—and have been for several decades.

at this through squinted eyes, I find myself stumbling back a step or two. My heart is racing, and I'm embarrassed that I haven't looked more closely at this before. Right here, in my own American backyard, it seems to me that we are trending back to a similar dynamic as in Victorian England—and have been for several decades.

I began my exploration of this idea by putting up a trial

balloon on Facebook, asking my diverse group of friends and acquaintances for current examples of economic injustice and criminalizing of poverty. Within minutes, we had a bitter array of prejudicial policies. Out of my 1500+ Facebook friends, just a small group chimed in. I'm not judging. I might not have chimed in myself before looking more intently into Wassail songs. There was mention of states where groceries are still taxed, which—like the coins for which the wassailers sang—could mean the difference between ample nutrition to sustain healthy living and sickness or even death if you are poor. Another law that disproportionately affects the poor is the driver's responsibility fee, where the driver's license is suspended or revoked after certain offenses, leaving some people with limited or no means to get to their jobs. People with ample financial resources are able to pay for alternate transportation, but for the poor, this translates to no job, no money, no help to get to work, and, therefore, no pulling themselves up by the bootstraps.

In another example, we see a parallel to Old England's tradition of the well-off keeping the poor wanting. I'm speaking of the Supreme Court decision that allows employers to demand that employees sign a mandatory arbitration clause as a condition of employment, effectively signing away their right, under the National Labor Relations Act, to join together with other workers for mutual aid or protection. This prevents employees from banding together to sue an unscrupulous employer for things like wage theft and discrimination, forcing a worker to go to arbitration with an arbitrator who is usually chosen by the employer. The employee must cover the legal costs themselves. This leaves low-wage earners less likely and less able to seek justice for themselves. If

How is this different from Victorian England when the wealthy also controlled the law and didn't care about the poor?

———

they do take the risk, they will likely face an arbitrator who is biased toward the employer, and will unlikely recoup lost income. How is this different from Victorian England when the wealthy also controlled the law and didn't care about the poor? Justice Ruth Bader Ginsberg called the decision by the Supreme Court "egregiously wrong" and in her dissent said that the right to join together with other workers isn't worth much if that right must be given up in order for the worker to get the job.

Here's another one: every day, more than 450,000 people in the United States who have not been convicted of any crime are put under lock and key in jails because they don't have the financial ability to pay bail. In the United States, we have a presumption of innocence until proven guilty. If you are well off, you are usually allowed to wait for your trial while sleeping in your bed and continuing to work at your job. If you are poor and unable to pay the bail, you are imprisoned in a jail cell, losing money and comfortable sleeping conditions—not to mention the presence of your loved ones—while the days, weeks, and months pass before your trial date and judgement by your jury of peers takes place. This reminds me of how the Dickens family was imprisoned for being in debt. Charles Dickens was haunted all his life by the terrifying memories of his childhood years spent working in a dangerous, rat-infested bootblacking workhouse to help his family get out of debt and out of jail.

The great explorer and adventurer, Sir Henry Morton Stanley, spent most of his childhood in an abusive workhouse where he had no choice but to steel himself against the daily physical torture and the psychological torture of watching his workhouse friends be beaten, sometimes to death. In his memoir, Stanley remembers how he thought some of his talented mates would do well for themselves when they were adults, but he was bitterly disappointed to see that—in spite of natural gifts many of the boys possessed—the years spent in the workhouse seemed to have beaten the spirit out of them. Sir Henry Morton Stanley and Charles Dickens were rare examples of spat-upon "workhouse brats," as they were commonly called, who, against all odds, found their way to success and fulfillment after such imprisonment for which they did nothing to deserve and out of which they were powerless to raise themselves. I am left wondering how much richer our world would be if spirits weren't broken in jails and figurative workhouses due to a lack of human kindness on a societal level. How many more delightful ideas, discoveries, and problems solved might we have if we didn't turn a blind eye to the plight of the poor? Might the world be better served if we looked at the poor not as a class of people to be punished or largely ignored except for tokens at Christmastime, but as a mass of untold potential to be lifted and given a chance to excel? I imagine them holding the wassail bowl out for us and saying "Waes Hael!" How can we say "Drink Hael" to them? We can toast their health by going to the voting booth and supporting policies that don't punish them for being poor.

CHAPTER 11

The Hallelujah Chorus

The Kingdom of this World

Hallelujah!
For the Lord God Omnipotent reigneth.
The kingdom of this world
is become the Kingdom of our Lord,
and of His Christ,
and He shall reign forever and ever.
King of Kings and Lord of Lords,
and he shall reign forever and ever.
Hallelujah!

Music: George Frideric Handel, from *The Messiah*, 1742
Words: Book of Revelation 19:6, 11:15, 19:16

There is a common, resilient thread I'd like to consider in this chapter. It connects George Frideric Handel, an American sea captain named Thomas Coram, Charles Dickens, thousands of abandoned children, and The Hallelujah Chorus itself. I call that thread "Comeback Kid." George Frideric Handel is considered one of the world's greatest artistic giants of all time, and *The Messiah*, of which The Hallelujah Chorus is a section, is widely considered his most acclaimed piece of work. However, in 1742, while Handel was conducting the second night of its London debut, when the Hallelujah Chorus started, the noise he heard behind him made him nervous. It sounded like people were getting out of their seats and leaving! Handel was virtually blind at this point in his life and couldn't see the people clearly.

Many years earlier, when he was still a child in Halle, Germany, Handel's father discouraged him from studying music. He went to law school, but he was sure it wasn't his calling. It's not clear whether he flunked out or merely withdrew from the school early. What is clear, is that he had a heart for music, and felt that he had God-given musical talents. It was his ardent intent to express his faith through music. At 18 years old, he moved to Hamburg and began to write operas with some success. Handel's love of God, music, and theatre came together when he moved to

Italy and wrote two theatrical religious concert works that garnered him the title "King of the Oratorios." In fact, by the age of 25, he was considered the most successful composer in all of Europe. Handel had always loved the English language and admired London theatre above all of the other theatre meccas. When invitations started coming from English writers, directors, and benefactors, he was delighted to move to England, where he became a naturalized citizen and lived for the rest of his life. It was in England that he saw the pinnacle of his success. He became artistically, commercially, and financially successful beyond his wildest dreams.

I've seen, so many times in my life, that as far in one direction as the pendulum swings, it seems it swings as far in the other, and George Handel was about to undergo a reversal of fortune. He was plagued with ill health. He'd had several strokes before he was even 40 years old. His body was becoming more and more crippled with rheumatism, and he was losing his eyesight. He spent all of his money in search of cures and doctors who might be able to help him. He even risked a crude and unsuccessful surgery on his eyes. Nothing helped. He became destitute, depressed, and creatively blocked. By the time he was 56 years old, he was blind, barely able to walk, and seemingly forgotten by the world that had put him on a pedestal and

By the time he was 56 years old, he was blind, barely able to walk, and seemingly forgotten by the world that had put him on a pedestal and crowned him king years earlier.

———

crowned him king years earlier. The wolf was at his door, and the most successful composer of his time feared he would soon be in debtors' prison.

Then, quite suddenly, the clouds opened and the finger of God seemed to reach through and touch George Frideric Handel on the forehead. Handel received, on the very same day, two very welcome pieces of mail. One was a letter from the Duke of Devonshire, inviting him to come to Ireland to write a series of benefit concerts, and the other was from a creative friend, handing over to him an idea for a biblical oratorio. For the first time in years, Handel felt a creative spark. He accepted both enthusiastically, and set about ferociously writing what we now know as *The Messiah*. He finished the "Christmas" section in seven days, and the whole piece was completed in 23 days. He debuted a modestly produced performance of it in Dublin on April 13, 1742, and word of Handel's amazing comeback spread like wildfire all through Europe.

The London debut was scheduled for just a few months later. English society was so eager to see it that the first few performances were sold out. King George II attended the second night. It is said that the king was so emotionally struck by Handel's work that when the first strains of the Hallelujah Chorus sounded, he was moved up and out of his seat! Well, you know the rule: When the king stands, everybody stands! And so, the whole audience rose to their feet in the middle of the performance as well. Imagine how unsettling that rustling behind him that must've been to Handel as he forced himself to continue to conduct the orchestra and chorus of singers! He must've been awfully relieved to learn that the commotion had everything to do with the king's astonished approval. That event made quite an impression, and to this day, the tradition continues for the audience to rise for the Hallelujah Chorus!

Three years earlier, while Handel was still creatively blocked, living on "the wrong side of London" and afraid of dying shriveled up in debtors' prison, an American sea captain was realizing a humanitarian dream come true on the other side of London. When the stern, salty-but-big-hearted Captain Thomas Coram retired from the sea and began to spend more time in London, he became very concerned with the state of her streets, where he saw human babies dying on top of piles of trash.

It's true that, as often illustrated by Dickens, from

his personal experience, London possessed scores of children dying or hustling to survive by begging, prostitution, scavenging in the river mud, pickpocketing, or risking their lives in the workhouses doing dangerous work in unsafe conditions with cruel taskmasters.

It seems that as the urbanization of England grew, the agricultural way of life was ruined and homelessness and births of illegitimate children increased. The problem had gotten so out of hand that it had bankrupted the parish relief system, leaving London a horrific scene of abandoned children, murdered babies, and despairing adults trying to find the means to stay alive.

At the beginning of the 17th century, children were dying at a hair-raising rate: one in three babies died before the age of two. Of those who survived, one in two died before they grew to be 15 years old. You may remember how, in *A Christmas Carol*, Scrooge asks the gentlemen soliciting alms for the poor on Christmas Eve if the workhouses are still in operation. The death rate of the workhouse children was 90%.

The death rate of the workhouse children was 90%.

There was a workhouse in one Westminster parish where only one in 500 children survived their workhouse experience!

You may ask, "Where were their mothers?" As this crisis

continued accelerating, a writer at that time, John Brownlow, wrote of the infanticide that arose from what he saw as a twisted morality in which weak young women were seduced by men who made false promises to them and then left them disgraced, with a fatherless child, and without resources with which to take care of it. And the worst of it was that neither the woman who made a grave mistake (with the missing father) nor the innocent child were shown human compassion.

The fact was that for single mothers, both the baby and the mother were in a very dangerous, uncertain position. If the baby died at birth, the mother would've been suspected of murder and arrested. Mothers who were found guilty were executed. Even if they were acquitted, their lives would've been left in shambles, and finding employment or prospects for marriage would've been greatly reduced, simply because of the accusation. And so, there was a sharp increase in abandoned babies being left in hospitals, churches, and workhouses.

Captain Thomas Coram had no children of his own and felt deeply for these forgotten children— these foundlings who had no advocate to afford them a sporting chance in life. He decided to do what he could to be their benefactor. In 1722, he began a petition to the king to grant a royal charter that would establish a hospital for these children to house them and look out for their maintenance and education. England didn't have such charities, and since the well-off looked at poverty as a moral failing of those affected, it was a great deal of hard work for Coram to persuade people of influence to sign on to his "darling project." But he persisted, and 17 years later, on August 14, 1739, he had enough signatures of people of "quality and distinction" to petition King George II to grant a "Royal Charter establishing the Hospital for the Maintenance of Exposed and Deserted Young Children." The king signed it, and the great seal was affixed to it on October 17, 1739. The great seal was designed by Coram himself and depicted Pharaoh's daughter finding the foundling Moses in the bulrushes. In a speech he gave to the president of the new hospital, Coram said, "The long and melancholy experience of this nation has too demonstrably shewn, with what barbarity tender infants have been exposed and destroyed for want of proper means of preventing the disgrace and succoring the necessities of their parents."

Coram and the Foundling Hospital became a model and example of charity in England. Only 13 years later, in 1752, novelist Henry Fielding wrote: "Charity is in fact the very characteristic of this nation at this time – I believe we may challenge the whole world to parallel the examples which we have of late given of this sensible, this noble, this Christian virtue."

The Foundling Hospital was England's first children's charity and was looked upon as one of the most remarkable institutions in England. In fact, it became the home for more than 27,000 children for the entirety of their childhoods.

There was a time when the English government carried the expense, but that meant that they could make the rules, and the governors of the hospital couldn't persuade the powers that be that their rules were harming the children. Then Coram made a brilliant move. He rejected government funds and rules and brought on some of the brightest artists of the day to donate their talents to the hospital which would draw the wealthy to events there to benefit the hospital. If you visit the Foundling Museum, in Bloomsbury, London, you will see exquisite paintings by William Hogarth, Francis Hayman, Emma Brownlow King, and others beautifying the

If you visit the Foundling Museum, in Bloomsbury, London, you will see exquisite paintings by William Hogarth, Francis Hayman, Emma Brownlow King, and others beautifying the walls.

walls. The art donated to the hospital is still bringing inspiration to many where it historically brought inspiration and hope to its residents and funds to keep the establishment operating.

One such artist was George Frideric Handel. Like Coram, he had no children of his own, but he certainly understood suffering. Having lost his own father at age 12, he had such a heart for these suffering children that once he became involved with the hospital, he enjoyed a long and productive relationship with it for the rest of his life. In 1749, after his comeback, he gave a concert of vocal and instrumental music at the hospital. The proceeds went toward finishing the hospital chapel. Significantly, the concert included an anthem that Handel crafted specifically for the hospital. It was titled "Blessed are They That Considereth the Poor." Some parts of *The Messiah* are incorporated into it, and it became the hospital's official anthem.

On May 1, 1750, Handel conducted the first of many performances of *The Messiah* that he would present to benefit the hospital. These benefits were so popular that the tickets requested that the gentlemen should not wear their swords and the ladies their hooped skirts to make room for the large audience that was expected. The concerts sold out, and more concerts were added, and Handel was brought on as a governor of the hospital. He donated the organ to the chapel, and his performances raised a tremendous amount of money for the benefit of the establishment. For the next 17 years, Handel conducted *The Messiah* at the hospital annually at Easter time until he was virtually blind and conducted his last one in May 1754. Even then, he attended every performance of *The Messiah* at the hospital until his death in April 1759.

The Hallelujah Chorus was played at Handel's funeral. Sadly, after Handel's death, people stopped performing *The Messiah*. About a century went by with it being all but forgotten. Then it made its comeback during the Victorian era, when it became a favorite annual music event in Protestant and Catholic churches. Once again, it became so popular that organizations recognized its capacity for fundraising. With Queen Victoria's love of Christmas carols, Prince Albert's German Christmas traditions in the palace, and the illustrations of the royal family celebrating around a Christmas tree in the newspapers, came a longer season of celebrating Christmas, more charitable attitudes at Christmastime, and greater fundraising prospects, and so *The Messiah* found itself a fixture in not

Sadly, after Handel's death, people stopped performing **The Messiah.**

only the Easter season, but also the Christmas holiday traditions we still enjoy today.

Between 1739 and 1955, the foundlings of Thomas Coram's Hospital, along with the art, music, and chapel, touched the lives of so many. One of those people was Charles Dickens himself. Dickens is, indeed, a comeback kid.

Dickens knew what a childhood should be like. His first few years of life showed him love, care, relative comfort and even two living parents. He had enough food to eat and was able to attend school and learn to read and write, among other useful subjects. However, the tide turned for his family, as happens to families everywhere, even today. I told you a little bit about Charles Dickens' experience in a workhouse. Now I will tell you more. In 1824, when young Charles Dickens was 12 years old, his family found themselves overcome with debt.

Charles was forced to drop out of school and be sent away to work, during the weekdays, at a boot-blacking workhouse, joining the rest of his family in a debtors' prison on the weekends. It was at this bleak point in Dickens' life that he learned, first hand, the unspeakable reality that scores of other English children had known for over a hundred years. Dickens had been so terrified by his experience in the blacking warehouse, with rats swarming amid dangerous conditions, that he wasn't able to bring himself to talk about it to anyone, except his biographer, John Forster (*The Life of Charles Dickens*), late in his life. When his family paid their debt and had the opportunity to take Charles out of the workhouse, much to his horror and despair, his mother was against the idea—a burning grief he would hold in his heart for the rest of his life. He asked, out loud, of Forster, how he "could have been so easily cast away at such an age." The most autobiographical of Dicken's works is

He asked, out loud, of Forster, how he "could have been so easily cast away at such an age."

David Copperfield. In it, he wrote, "I had no advice, no counsel, no encouragement, no consolation, no assistance, no support, of any kind, from anyone, that I can call to mind..."

So, it was that early in life, he fully identified with the poor, disadvantaged people facing unfair and cruel conditions with no advocates to speak on their behalf or protect them. As we all know, he turned that around. In spite of not being able to finish school, Charles Dickens became one of the greatest writers of all time, wordsmithing his gift into a magnifying glass and shining a glaring light onto the social injustices of the times in such a way as to cause people to open their hearts and minds and call for change. During his adult years, his fame and wild popularity was as large in America as anywhere, and he capitalized on that by publicly quoting newspaper articles about runaway slaves who had been disfigured by their cruel masters. He openly condemned slavery and likened the abolition of it in America with the emancipation of the poor in England.

In the 1840s, when Dickens lived on Doughty Street with his young, growing family, he became involved in the nearby Foundling Hospital, and its chapel, which became his home on Sundays. He was keenly aware of the contributions to the hospital made by Handel a hundred years prior, including the chapel organ along which he would sing from his rented pew. The foundlings inspired characters in his work, such as the title character in *Oliver Twist*, Tattycoram in *Little Dorrit* (who was a portrayal of a foundling growing up in the hospital) and in *No Thoroughfare*, the little one dropped off at that hospital who is reclaimed, Walter Wilding.

An article Dickens wrote in a publication called *Household Words* in March 1853 drew favorable attention to the hospital. It was titled "Received a Blank Child" after a reference to the form that was required to be filled out for each child admitted into the hospital. It reads very much like any of his novels with colorful descriptions and unique turns of phrase, as he describes the happy children, how much they loved their teachers, how they were inspired by the art on the walls, and the music they heard played on Handel's organ. Notably, he witnessed and memorialized the children joyfully playing instruments and bellowing Handel's Hallelujah Chorus through the hallways.

No less impressive were the comebacks of these children, growing up with diminished chances at succeeding in life. Not having parents, being labeled illegitimate, and having to get in step with a harsh regime was very difficult and, at times, unbearable to these children. Being a resident in the Foundling Hospital was a rough start that no child would ask for, but some bright spots and compassionate people brought them joy and hope and lifted them. The Foundling Hospital raised, taught, and maintained abandoned children for over 200 years, ceasing most of its operations in the 1950s. In contrast to the children in workhouses, the majority of the children who grew up in the Foundling Hospital went on to lead happy, successful lives with stable families of their own.

In interviews with adults who had grown up in the Foundling Hospital, the music stood out as a highlight, transporting them out of their painful childhood lives, temporarily. One of them went so far as to call his time in jazz band "pure heaven," but many of them went on to professions in music or continued to be enriched by it in a recreational way all through their lives. One former resident said, "Music did play a major role, and Sundays were the best day. I remember the peace and serenity of the chapel, and the organ and choir. It wasn't until I was 14 or 15 that I ever admitted something was beautiful. I joined the choir and reveled in that. It was another world, away from the Foundling Hospital."

Another former student recalled the time she was in the Foundling Hospital's infirmary at age 12. She was very frightened after an asthma attack, when she heard a particular piece of music over the loud speaker. She described the event as "a new world" opening up for her; a pivotal moment in her life, "a recognition that there would always be a never-ending supply of good things..." At age 24, she went on to say, "I had another moment of revelation, when I realized that music touched the center of my life, and everything would always be all right."[1]

REFLECTIONS

Just as with Christmas, not everyone, Christian or not, feels joyful on Easter every year. Some years, we feel the weight of Good Friday for months on end.

---

1 Pugh, Gilliam. *London's Forgotten Children: Thomas Coram and the Foundling Hospital.* London: The History Press; 2011.

As Holy Saturday and Easter Sunday arrive, we try to punch through the burial cloth. We try to forget the bloody, swollen, bruised images and agonizing outcries to God. We try to suppress the admission that we ourselves are trying to roll away that ponderous stone and see that God is all-powerful; that God is bigger than our troubles; that God loves us so much that He would take on the grief of His precious Son being brutally tortured in the worst kind of way, and then with one supernatural, glorious stroke, heal the wounds, and with a white blast of breath, exclaim "Ha!" at death. But that stone is massive. We can't budge that stone on our own, and it's hard to admit that we are trying to be so self-reliant when we have heard that we have only to knock, and the door will be opened.

Some years are like that. I had a year like that. My teenaged son had become a stranger to me and all who loved him. Things were so bad that I didn't think I had the strength or faith to be away from him long enough to rehearse or sing with the choir for the Easter service. But I pulled out the obligatory spring dress from the closet. I put on the best face I could. I put heroic effort into making it a special day for him. Although I couldn't compel him to come with me, I went to church and smiled my best smiles. I admired the Easter lilies and said "Hallelujah!" I put my whole body, mind, and strength into pushing that stone away,

I put my whole body, mind, and strength into pushing that stone away, but it stood fixed and unyielding, and I felt Friday's shroud weighing heavily over any joy of Easter I might've felt.

---

but it stood fixed and unyielding, and I felt Friday's shroud weighing heavily over any joy of Easter I might've felt.

Yes, some years are extremely challenging, but even the chains of mundane, everyday disappointments can be heavy. I'm writing this on Easter Sunday. Yesterday was Holy Saturday, and I have to admit that, although this Easter weekend is 99% better than last year's for me, that 1% had me less than joyful as I parked my car and entered our church choir room to rehearse today's music. But then, something happened. As I sang the Hallelujah Chorus and other Easter pieces with my fellow choristers, I was suddenly aware of a change that had taken place within me. I was more than joyful! It shouldn't have been a surprise to me. This is one of the key ideas I've been exploring with Christmas carols. Music is healing. Taking in music with others is elating; experiencing divinely inspired music with others is transcending!

To *transcend* is to triumph over the restrictive aspects of something: to go beyond the limits of something. Everywhere I look, I see how divinely inspired music can help us transcend our feelings of worry and despair and also our childhood situations and what we perceive as our limited power to affect change in our families and even in the world. There is a powerful spirit alive in that music. That spirit seems to shine with a brighter light at Christmas and Easter time. There is Christmas in Easter and Easter in Christmas, and the spirit that electrifies them both invites us—no, *more* than invites us—charges us to open our hearts to that holiest of spirits and connect with each other through it.

I think Dickens said "yes" to that charge. I can imagine him, sitting in his pew at the Foundlings Hospital Chapel, his boot-blacking workhouse inner child feeling that electric charge connecting him with the parentless waifs sitting there with him, in that blessed space, which was made possible by the funds brought in by that divinely inspired work, born out of the ashes of ill health and poverty, performed under the baton of none other than that other fellow sufferer, Handel's crippled hand. What connection! What comebacks! What spirit! Hallelujah!

CHAPTER 12

Why It Works

I hope you've enjoyed reading about some of the interesting history behind a few of the world's most beloved carols and how they've extracted my curiosity and inspiration to apply the wisdom to life today. There are so many things to learn about any one of the carols that I have returned to them time and time again, finding new histories to be discovered, applications to be made, and questions to be asked from different angles. I've been doing this for years now, and I am continually surprised, always inspired, and sometimes downright shocked at the way Christmas carols have been a vehicle for the divine to touch mortals such as us in both dramatic and mundane settings.

As I said at the beginning of this book, I knew during the first week—the first day even—that this journey into the carols was working to revive my damaged Christmas spirit. But why was it working? I was just so happy that it was that I didn't think to ask myself that question right away. Like a tourist in an exotic land, I trekked along, wide-eyed and slack-jawed for about four years before it occurred to me to attempt to figure it out. The reason the question even presented itself was because the answer hit me between the eyes one day.

I knew that my spirit had received a blow. I knew that a traumatic experience had shaken my faith in my fellow humans and damaged something inside me that normally would have allowed me to be lifted in holiday joy. And now I knew that making new discoveries about Christmas carols had somehow not only remedied my blocked spirit but had, indeed, opened the floodgates to free-flowing holiday joy.

As a thespian, I've been fascinated with human behavior for as long as I can remember.

As a thespian, I've been fascinated with human behavior for as long as I can remember. As a professional acting coach,

I've coached many people to prepare for their auditions that have landed them roles in film, television, Broadway, tours, and other theatrical productions. I'm told that one of the reasons these actors call upon me is because I have the ability to put them in touch with emotions, thoughts, and imagery necessary to make their auditions come to life. One of my favorite devices with which to do this is "sense-memory."

We've all experienced sense-memories in our lives. These are memories and emotions that are triggered through our senses. Have you ever visited a place and been immediately transported back to a particular time or event in your life? Perhaps it was the smell of an oil tank system heating a room of shellacked woodwork, or your grandfather's aftershave, that makes your heart quicken. As I write this, I can imagine those very smells, combined with boiling potatoes, and suddenly I can hear my grandmother's laugh, and I can see my grandparents' dimly lit basement just down the stairs from the kitchen, where my siblings and I played hide and seek, knowing we would soon join her, my grandfather, uncle, and parents for a delicious meal. Their house wasn't what you'd call a children's wonderland. We often complained about being bored there, but truth be told, that caused us to spend more inventive time playing together, and that was special. That brought us closer. That made us love each other more. When I think of the smell of oil heat, I can easily recall that feeling of childhood love and fun between us siblings.

I had an elderly, dear and funny eighth grade English teacher named Mrs. Miller. There are many things I've forgotten from the chapters of the Strunk and White book on the principles of composition, but I think I could lose my memory to old age and still remember what a direct object is because of Mrs. Miller. Mrs. Miller was tall and thin, always dressed in feminine chiffon dresses, and she smiled at us through a closed, determined mouth that made her bright coral lips disappear. Her eyes would start to gleam as she wound up her arm and threw things at us.

She'd yell, "Mrs. Miller threw the book! What's the direct object?"

"The book! The book!" we respond, as we shielded our faces behind our arms.

"Mrs. Miller threw the pencil! What's the direct object?"

"The pencil, the pencil!"

She loved us, and she was extravagant in her praise and expectations of us. She wore way too much perfume. It was called Heaven Scent, and we could tell when she was coming around a corner in the hallways because we could smell her first! When I smell that fragrance, or one like it, I stand a little taller, smile a little wider, and feel a little smarter.

Fragrances of soaps, flowers, foods, the brand of coffee your parents had percolating when company was visiting, sulfuric smells of stagnant ponds, decaying leaves, wet dogs, the smell of your yard or neighborhood right after a spring rain, lotions, incense—the list is endless—might all trigger your emotions.

When I smell that fragrance, or one like it, I stand a little taller, smile a little wider, and feel a little smarter.

All of our senses have this ability to unlock memories and feelings within us. Sometimes the feelings and memories are those we would like to avoid and forget altogether! For instance, the smell of a certain fruity kids' cereal activates my gag reflex and makes my nose contract. I can so easily remember my father putting a bowl of what was then my favorite cereal in front of me one Saturday morning. I was about seven years old and my mother was working at the hospital. I didn't feel well, but my father was a stickler for making us eat what was on our plate, or in this case, in my bowl. I dutifully started spooning it into my mouth. I only got about three swallows in before I was running to that other bowl—the one in the bathroom—and seeing that same cereal in front on me in that. I'm sure the taste of this cereal would also be an effective trigger, but I have no desire to ever taste it again. Let's not dwell on that one! I know that, for some, the smell of mink oil and rubber bands brings back happy memories of fathers or other mentors showing them how to break in a new baseball glove in anticipation of a little league season.

If you were any kind of a scout or if you've ever camped or spent time around a campfire, the taste of graham crackers, Hershey's chocolate, and roasted marshmallows will most likely be a wonderful sense memory for you. Although I've made them, countless times, with my own children in our living room, in front of our fireplace, that taste still turns me into a six-year-old girl who was scared to be at sleepaway camp, but who was surprised and delighted to be taken under the wing of a much older girl, around a campfire on the last night. She had spent time that week making me a log boat onto which she wrote an encouraging note. We had all made such boats to exchange. Mine was quite simple. I don't remember who it went to. But I remember that this girl had made hers intentionally for me. This campfire experience was the last night of our stay, and after we exchanged boats, sang songs, roasted marshmallows, and ate s'mores, we put little candles in the boats and floated them down a river. Today, the taste of s'mores still makes me inhale a quick sensation of wonder at unexpected acceptance and generosity.

Conversely, the tastes of certain medicines and antiseptic mouthwashes may bring back a feeling of being sick. If you were ever forced to sit at the table until you'd finished your cold, smelly Brussel sprouts, after the rest of the family had been excused, the taste of them may make you feel lonely and full of dread.

The sight of a sunset behind the silhouette of Florida palm trees makes me feel romantic. I think I was experiencing the dawn of my romantic consciousness, and probably had a big crush on someone when my family took a lovely vacation in Clearwater. That image still feels like paradise to me. The sight of morning sun on a red barn near wheat fields gives me the feeling of newfound independence: as a senior in high school I would cross the street from my school and make pastel chalk renderings of the old barn there. Not only was I independent in my study, but my parents were giving me more independence as well, as I prepared to graduate and drove myself to my job after school as well. Listening to Billy Joel's album, *The Stranger*, gives me that same feeling, because the car I drove to work had an eight-track tape player in it, and one of the only eight-track tapes we owned was that one, as eight-track tapes were an outmoded technology by then. I admit I was lucky to have such a wonderful album be one of the few to which I had access! The sight of a lightening-filled sky, crocuses popping up out of the earth, the ocean, sand dunes, a favorite old children's book cover, a particular crayon from a Crayola 64-count collection, school lockers, a tetherball pole, a holy water font, and countless other images you either lay eyes on or picture in your mind's eye can trigger feelings and memories.

Have you ever noticed what it feels like in early September, as the seasons are changing from summer to fall, and you put on an autumn jacket or sweater, and feel the sun and air in a different way on your skin? Does it make you feel a sense of anticipation that is reminiscent of the excitement or maybe fear of the first day of school? This is one my favorites, because I loved the first day of school and the new beginning and the chance to put my best foot forward it represented. The feeling and act of rubbing sand-paper on wood may bring back memories and good feelings associated with making a pinewood derby car with dad. The smell of model paint might do the same. If dad cared a little too much about the com-petition and commandeered the project or placed too much emphasis on winning, feelings of anxiety or sadness might be triggered instead. Although the moment might've seemed ordinary to us at the time, if there was even subconscious emotion present, our amazing minds may have imprinted these memories and emotions onto our perceptions of these sights, sounds, tastes, smells, and touch experiences.

Our sense experiences that imprint so strongly give us the ability to immediately recall and bring to the forefront of our minds memories and feelings we haven't felt or thought of in years. Some of these are hard to re-create, but sometimes we find ourselves suddenly stepping into such an atmosphere and experiencing this amazing phenomenon.

Sound is a powerful sense memory activator. The sound of a gentle summer breeze through sheer curtains and a window screen, along with the grinding and whirring of a distant excavator, puts me in my childhood bedroom having just woken from an afternoon nap in our neighborhood which was still being developed at the time. I must've been three years old. It's one of my earliest memories. I don't know why it attached itself the way it did, but it must've been a good memory, because it brings with it a feeling of contentedness; a rested grogginess of wanting to go to the dining room where I have the idea that my mother is smiling and has a peanut butter and jelly sandwich on a plate for me, with pear slices on the side. On the other side of that coin is the way the sound of a sewing machine tightens my stomach with impending doom. I think my mother may have summoned me to a scolding while sewing a time or two! The sound of chalk making quick strokes on a blackboard may make your heart start pounding the way it did before an elementary school arithmetic test. The sound of a motor on a fishing boat may hold a full heart of fishing memories with a loved one for you.

The sound of a motor on a fishing boat may hold a full heart of fishing memories with a loved one for you.

You may have noticed that I save the senses of touch and sound for last. That is because what hit me between the eyes was the realization that sound and touch sense memories are powerfully at play when we hear and sing Christmas carols. Looking at the text and images as we research the carols adds the sense of sight to the mix as well. Sense memory is the secret ingredient that makes this process work so well. I had heard carols since I was 10 months old. I heard them in church, on the radio, on my parents' record player, I learned them at school for our Christmas concerts, I sang them with friends in school busses on field trips, I heard them on the television, next to our Christmas tree as I watched Christmas specials. I not only heard them, but I sang them while I heard them. The physical vibration of them coming into my ears met with the vibration of my vocal chords resonating through my body—we are experiencing and activating our senses of hearing and feeling when we are listening to and singing carols. Christmas carols activate powerful sense memories for me and so many others! That's wonderful, right? Except it's tragic when something damaging attaches itself to these treasured triggers. And that's what happened to me, while I was struggling with my faith in humanity. So, what did studying the carols do to change that?

Quite simply, unbeknownst to me at the time, I took sense memories—what I now call "spirit triggers"—and reset them at a time of year when I had no expectation of them. As I looked at and learned histories of things all around each carol and listened to and sang the carols with a new mindset, I was filled with a new excitement and wonder-filled emotion. When the next holiday season rolled along, and I heard or sang or saw the title of each carol I'd studied, I felt like an overachieving kid in the classroom, shooting my hand up to tell everybody what I discovered! Once I realized how sense memory was resetting damaged holiday triggers for me, I took fuller advantage of the idea. I purchased an essential oil diffuser and found a few different oils to diffuse while reading and writing about the carols. I grew up Catholic, with

Frankincense being burned in church on holy days. I have found that diffusing Frankincense essential oil while I'm writing puts me in a more focused, higher state of mind. I've been known to enjoy a candy cane while reading and writing about the carols, and I took full advantage of my yearly tradition of steaming plum puddings, taking in that very specific aroma while learning more about the carols.

You have already started this process by reading this book! How do you feel? One thing I feel sure of is that you will never hear or sing the carols in this book in the same way again. I'd like to encourage you to continue with this process by doing your own independent study. In fact, I'll make it easy for you.

When I first started, I wasn't thinking about a particular process as much as simply spending time researching a carol each week. History was not a subject at which I had ever excelled, but in spite of that fact, I found myself spending more time than I had to spare down the carol rabbit hole! It began to feel like a luxury, the time for which I couldn't always budget. But I reminded myself

I reminded myself that this was not merely a luxury. This was much-needed nourishment for my spirit.

that this was not merely a luxury. This was much-needed nourishment for my spirit.

I realized that I was writing the inspirations in journals, on calendars, and in greeting cards, and eventually created work pages and calendars to help me keep my process quick, simple, and fun. You can find my *Defeating Scrooge* calendars, workbooks, greeting cards, and more at: www.ismileny.com. I have included one week's worth of workbook pages at the end of this book. You may download unlimited, free workbook page templates on the website as well. This is how I started. Three-hole punch them and put them in a three-ring binder and start your own journey.

And please write to me and let me know how it's going! I'd love to hear your stories!

CHAPTER 13

The Process

Each step of the process is explained more fully on the workbook pages, but here is the process simply put:

DAY ONE: Choose a carol and let it be easy on your mind as you go through your day. If you know any of the words, sing them to yourself, or find an online or other version you can listen to.

DAY TWO: Read through the lyrics, and let the words linger in your mind as you go through your day. Muse over your understanding of the lyrics and be on the lookout for anything in your life or environment to which the lyrics could apply.

DAY THREE: Research the meaning of any words in the lyrics that you do not fully understand. Alternately, research the etymology of words that interest you. When was the carol written? Did the words have different meaning back then than they do now? Who is the lyricist?

DAY FOUR: Who is the composer? Were the lyrics written at the same time as the music? Where did the lyricist and composer live? Who was their audience? Research brief biographies of them.

DAY FIVE: What was going on in the country of the carol's origin at the time it was being written? Can you find or imagine the circumstances that may have inspired the carol's author(s) to write this particular carol?

DAY SIX: Jump ahead in history. Research the history of the carol since the time it was written. Can you find stories of incidents when this carol touched the lives of people in a meaningful way?

DAY SEVEN: Briefly look at your notes from days 1 to 6. Do any of the discoveries you've made about this carol resonate with your current concerns in your personal life or broader world concerns? Sing or play the carol again. Notice how differently you feel about it than you did on day one!

CHAPTER 14

A List of Carols

Here is an incomplete list of carols to get you started. Do not limit yourself to this list; use any and all means you find to look for more.

A Holly Jolly Christmas
Ah, Bleak the Chill and Wintry Wind
All On a Christmas Morning
Angels We Have Heard on High
Away in a Manger
Bring a Torch, Jeannette Isabella
Candles of Hanukkah, Candles of Christmas
Carol of the Bells
Caroling, Caroling

The Christmas Song
Christmastime is Here
Deck the Hall
Ding Dong! Merrily on High
Do You Hear What I Hear?
Feliz Navidad
First Noel, The
Friendly Beasts
Frosty the Snowman
Fum, Fum, Fum
Glad Christmas Bells
Go Tell it On the Mountain
God Rest You Merry, Gentlemen
Good Christian Men, Rejoice
Good King Wenceslas
Hallelujah Chorus
Hanukah O Hanukah
Happy Hanukah
Hark! The Herald Angels Sing
Have Yourself a Merry Little Christmas
Here We Come A-Wassailing
Holly and the Ivy
I Have a Little Dreidel
I Heard the Bells on Christmas Day
I Saw Three Ships
I Wonder as I Wander
I'll Be Home For Christmas

It Came Upon the Midnight Clear
It's Beginning to Look a Lot Like Christmas
It's the Most Wonderful Time
Jingle Bells
Jolly Old Saint Nicholas
Joy to the World
Let it Snow!
Little Drummer Boy, The
Light the Candles of Freedom
Lo, How a Rose E'er Blooming
Lullay, Thou Little Tiny Child
O Christmas Tree
O Come, All Ye Faithful
O Holy Night
O Little Town of Bethlehem
Ocho Kandelikas
Pat A Pan
Rockin' Jingle Bell Rock
Rudolph
Santa Claus is Coming to Town
Silent Night!
Silver Bells
Snow
Twelve Days of Christmas
Up on the House-top
Wassail, Wassail
We Three Kings of Orient Are

We Wish You a Merry Christmas
We'll Dress the House
What Child is This?
While Shepherds Watched
White Christmas
Winter Wonderland

CHAPTER 15

Christmas Spirit Saver Workbook Pages

SATURDAY

Choose next week's carol:

_____

_____

PRAY

As early in the day as possible, ask for inspiration to find just the right carol for you at this very point and time in your life.

MEDITATE

Sit quietly and breathe deep, long breaths in and out. Try not to think of anything. If thoughts come to your mind, other than a Christmas carol–related thought, don't let yourself be bothered by it. Instead, just gently put the thought aside, knowing that it will be there for you to tend to later. Maintain this for 10 minutes or so.

CONSIDER

Has a carol presented itself to you? If not, you may want to refer to the List of Carols in the previous chapter for inspiration. As you look at the titles, see if a one jumps off the page at you. Record your thoughts, inspirations, and questions here:

_____

_____

_____

_____

_____

_____

_____

SING and/or LISTEN

If you know any of the words, sing them to yourself, or find an online or other version to which you can listen.

Record your thoughts, inspirations, and questions here:

_____

_____

_____

_____

_____

_____

_____

_____

LIVE YOUR LIFE

If no carol has beckoned you yet, let the titles linger at the back of your mind as you go through your day. If you need further inspiration, as it gets later in the day, look up the lyrics of a few of them, and see if they speak to you. Perhaps your breath will quicken at certain thoughts. Or maybe a lyric will remind you of something you are encountering in your present life.

MUSE

This day should be a day of musing, and letting a carol choose you if you will allow it.

If you happen to find yourself "on fire" or "in love" with the idea of a particular carol, and you are inspired to immerse yourself in it at once, then by all means, follow that instinct and research, consider, and write to your heart's content! Enjoy!

SUNDAY

PRAY

As early as possible in your day, Pray about your newly chosen carol.

Record any inspirations you receive from praying about your carol here:

_____

_____

_____

_____

_____

_____

MEDITATE

READ

Read through every word of the lyrics. (Google, Wikipedia, other online resources, or *A Christmas Caroler's Book of Christmas Lyrics.*)

Record any inspirations you receive from reading the lyrics here:

_____

_____

_____

_____

_____

_____

_____

LIVE WITH THE LYRICS

Let the words linger as you go through the first part of your day.

Record any inspirations here:

_____

_____

_____

_____

_____

_____

_____

_____

WORSHIP*

If you are able, go to your place of spiritual nourishment (church, temple, etc.).

If you are unable to physically go to such a place, spend some time watching, listening or reading spiritual content.

Be on the lookout for ways in which this content could tie into this week's carol.

Record any inspirations you receive about how this content could tie into your carol here:

---

* If you attend on Saturdays, then use this sheet, and practice this meditation on Saturday, or whichever your chosen day of religious observation is.

MONDAY

PRAY

As early as possible in your day, pray to find inspiration and meaning as you research the words of the carol's lyric, the date it was written, and the lyricist.

Record any inspirations you receive from praying about your carol here:

_____

_____

_____

_____

_____

_____

_____

MEDITATE

READ

Research the meaning of any words in the lyric of which you do not fully understand. You may want to research the etymology of words that interest you.

Record any inspirations you receive from reading about the words of the carol here:

_____

_____

_____

_____

_____

_____

When was the carol written? Did the words have different meaning back then than they do now?

Record any inspirations you receive from reading about the time in history when the carol was written here:

_____

_____

_____

_____

_____

_____

Who is the lyricist?

Record any inspirations you receive from reading about the lyricist of the carol here:

_____

_____

_____

_____

_____

_____

_____

TUESDAY

PRAY

As early as possible in your day, pray to find inspiration and meaning as you research the lives of the carol's composer and lyricist.

Record any inspirations you receive from praying about your carol here:

_____

_____

_____

_____

_____

MEDITATE

READ

Who is the composer of this carol?

Record any inspirations you receive from reading about the composer of the carol here:

_____

_____

_____

_____

_____

What was the relationship between the composer and lyricist?

Record any inspirations here:

_____

_____

_____

_____

_____

_____

Who were the composer and lyricist writing for? Who was their audience? What inspired them to write this carol?

Record any inspirations here:

_____

_____

_____

_____

_____

_____

_____

Look up biographies of the composer and lyricist. What were their lives like before and after they wrote this carol?

Record any inspirations here:

_____

_____

_____

_____

_____

_____

_____

WEDNESDAY

PRAY

As early as possible in your day, pray to find inspiration and meaning as you research the carol's country of origin and historical events happening at the time the carol was written.

Record any inspirations you receive from praying about your carol here:

_____

_____

_____

_____

_____

_____

MEDITATE

READ

Where did the carol's composer and lyricist live at the time they wrote the carol?

Record any inspirations here:

_____

_____

_____

_____

_____

_____

What was happening in that country at the time the carol was written?

Record any inspirations here:

_____

_____

_____

_____

_____

_____

Look for stories about or imagine the circumstances which might've inspired the carol's author(s) to write this carol.

Record any inspirations here:

_____

_____

_____

_____

_____

_____

THURSDAY

PRAY

As early as possible in your day, pray to find inspiration and meaning as your research the impact the carol has had in the world since it was written.

Record any inspirations you receive from praying about your carol here:

_____

_____

_____

_____

_____

_____

_____

MEDITATE

READ

Jump ahead. Research the history of the carol since the time it was written. Look for stories of incidents when this carol touched the lives of people in a meaningful way.

Record any inspirations here:

_____

_____

_____

_____

_____

FRIDAY

PRAY

As early as possible in your day, pray to find inspiration and meaning as you ponder what you've learned about the carol over the last six days and how it might apply to your life today.

Record any inspirations you receive from praying about your carol here:

_____

_____

_____

_____

_____

MEDITATE

READ

Look over your notes from the past six days. Do any of the discoveries you've made about this carol resonate with your current concerns in your personal life?

Record any inspirations you receive from reading about the composer of the carol here:

_____

_____

_____

_____

_____

_____

CONSIDER

Consider current events in world news you may have read about or heard on the radio, television or from people with whom you've come in contact. Can you find any wisdom from this carol that you can apply to these events?

Record any inspirations here:

_____

_____

_____

_____

_____

_____

SING!

Sing the carol to yourself. How does it feel different to you today that it did when you sang or listened to it six days ago?

Record any inspirations here:

_____

_____

_____

_____

_____

_____

ENJOY

Inhale the satisfaction of having begun this journey to revive and nurture your Christmas spirit. To continue your journey through the carols, visit www. ismileny.com where you may download unlimited complimentary Spirit Saver pages.

Remember, even old Ebenezer Scrooge cracked his cold, hard shell and let in the light of new inspirations. That solitary oyster of a character reset his holiday spirit triggers. He chose not to live without the joy of Christmas, and so can we! No matter what is going on in your life, may all of your Christmas seasons be joyful and triumphant!

About the Author

RENAE BAKER is professional singer, actor, speaker, and sometimes television and radio cohost, as well as founder and director of I S.M.I.L.E. in New York Productions and the I S.M.I.L.E. Movement. She has led this company of holiday carolers from the Broadway community since 1997 and they perform under the names: The Fabulous Fezziwigs, The Broadway CARE-olers, The Y'alltide Carolers, and the Currier & Ives Carolers. Her groups of carolers have performed at some of the most iconic sites in New York City, and are part of what makes the city so special during the holidays. Renae believes that

the true spirit of the holiday season transcends boundaries and that every December we have an opportunity to further the cause of world peace. She and her carolers perform in the most diverse city in the world and the surrounding tristate area, bringing people of different cultures, races, religions, orientations, and persuasions joyfully together in song.

Renae has been putting a cappella vocal groups together since her childhood in Michigan, and she holds a BFA in Musical Theatre from the University of Michigan. In addition to her leading and singing in her caroling groups, Renae is a public speaker on topics involving Christmas and the winter holidays. She also leads Spirit Saver workshops, which bring people together with carols as they explore and revive their Christmas spirits. These workshops are great for team building, increasing church membership, and are memorable, meaningful gatherings of friends and family.

Renae is also a sought-after acting coach, specializing in helping children; she has coached actors for their auditions, helping them land roles in Broadway, film, and television productions. Her ability to help people access their emotions is a key element to the process she created to help herself and others revive their holiday spirit. To contact Renae to schedule a coaching session, go to: www.thechildactorwhisperer.com.

For more information on how to book the carolers, a workshop, or schedule Renae to speak at your event, go to: www.ismileny.com.

If you enjoyed reading DEFEATING SCROOGE,
you can have the joyful sound of Renae's carolers
in your ears any time of year!

A New York Christmas S.M.I.L.E. and
A New York Hanukkah S.M.I.L.E.
can be found on CD Baby:

store.cdbaby.com/cd/anewyorkchristmassmile

store.cdbaby.com/cd/thefabulousfezziwigs

Renae's mission is to help people who struggle with holiday spirit for whatever reason or who simply want to add more meaning to their December holiday experiences. She speaks on a variety of holiday topics ranging from the annual controversy over holiday greetings to how music can build bridges of harmony between people and bring about more world peace.

Is your State of Spirit an S.O.S? Defeating Scrooge workshops to nurture and revive holiday spirit are offered all year long!

Great for:

- Team building
- Church events to playfully involve the community and increase membership
- Unforgettable gatherings of friends and family
- *And more!*

Live events available and DVD and online programs coming soon!

To book a live event, go to:

www.ismileinnewyorkproductions.com/book-your-event/

To see photos and videos, hear sound clips and to book
the I S.M.I.L.E. in New York carolers:

The Fabulous Fezziwigs

The Currier & Ives Carolers

or The Broadway CARE-olers, go to:

www.ismileny.com!

CPSIA information can be obtained
at www.ICGtesting.com
Printed in the USA
BVHW03*1615141018
529544BV00001B/1/P